Stargazing for Kids

An Introduction to Astronomy

Jonathan Poppele

Adventure Publications
Cambridge, Minnesota

Edited by Brett Ortler

Cover and book design by Jonathan Norberg

Credits continued on page 175

10 9 8 7 6 5 4 3
Stargazing for Kids
Copyright © 2022 by Jonathan Poppele
Published by Adventure Publications, an imprint of AdventureKEEN
310 Garfield Street South
Cambridge, Minnesota 55008
(800) 678-7006
www.adventurepublications.net
All rights reserved
Printed in the United States of America
ISBN 978-1-64755-134-6 (pbk.); 978-1-64755-135-3 (ebook)

Stargazing for Kids

An Introduction to Astronomy

Table of Contents

An Introduction to Astronomy

Have you ever looked up at the night sky filled with stars? Have you ever looked for patterns in the stars, or watched them move across the sky? Have you ever just gazed in amazement and wondered how far away they are? What they are made of? If there are other worlds out there somewhere? You're not alone.

Astronomy is the study of things beyond the Earth, like stars, planets, moons, comets, and galaxies. A person who studies astronomy is called an astronomer. Professional astronomers are scientists whose job it is to study objects in the sky. People who study the sky simply because they love it are amateur astronomers.

Although astronomy is the study of things beyond the Earth, most astronomy is done from Earth. This is where we live, after all. For thousands of years, people have been studying the cosmos by looking up into the night sky. You can do the same thing.

By learning a little about astronomy, you can become an amateur astronomer. You might even love it so much that you decide to study math and science in school and make astronomy your job one day.

There is a lot to explore. The universe is a big place. So let's get started.

MOVEMENT OF THE STARS AT NIGHT

We all know how the sun appears to move across the sky. It rises in the east, arcs across the southern sky, and sets in the west. This movement is the result of the Earth rotating on its axis. The spin of the Earth causes the stars to move across the sky in much the same way.

Star trails, looking north

Star trails, looking east

Each night, the stars move in a large circle around Polaris, the North Star. Stars that are close to Polaris make small circles and are visible all night. Stars that are farther from Polaris rise in the east and set in the west, just like the sun. To the south, stars rise in the southeast, trace a low arc in the sky, and set in the southwest.

As the Earth orbits around the sun, it faces different parts of the sky. Each night, stars will appear to rise and set about four minutes earlier than the night

Star trails, looking south

before. The four Sky Tours (page 107) in this book will show you stars that are easiest to see in each of the four seasons.

What Can I See?

You can see the effect of Earth's rotation and orbit yourself by observing how stars appear to move in the sky. Head out on a clear, dark evening after it's gotten dark enough to see some stars. Find a few bright stars in different parts of the sky (the brightest "stars" might actually be planets!), and note where you see them. Look for landmarks to help you remember. What direction are they? How high are they above the horizon? An hour later, head back out and look again. How much have the stars moved? Did some stars move more than others? Two weeks later, go out at the same time of night and look one more time. Where are the stars now?

Long exposure photographs of the night sky will show the movement of the stars. Instead of looking like points of light, the stars will look like "trails" across the sky. The shape of the

How our view of the constellations changes as Earth orbits the sun

trails are different depending on what direction we look. If you have a tripod and a camera that can take long exposures, you can try this for yourself.

TWILIGHT

When the sky is dark, we call it night. When the sun is up, we call it daytime. But the sky is also light just after sundown and just before sunrise. We call this time in between day and night twilight. When we head out to look at stars after sunset, we need to wait for the sky to get dark. We need to wait for the end of twilight. How long depends on what we want to see. There are three stages of twilight.

During civil twilight, the sky is bright enough that we can read without a light. Only the brightest stars and planets are visible. Civil twilight lasts for about half an hour after sunset.

Twilight progression: civil, nautical, astronomical, and full dark

During nautical twilight, brighter stars are visible. There is still a glow on the horizon near where the sun set. Nautical twilight lasts until about an hour after sunset.

During astronomical twilight, the entire sky appears dark, and faint stars are visible. In areas that suffer from light pollution, the sky is as dark as it will get. Astronomical twilight lasts until about an hour and a half after sunset. In areas with no light pollution, the dimmest stars, nebulae, and galaxies become visible after astronomical twilight ends.

LIGHT POLLUTION

A little more than 100 years ago, people could go outside every night and see thousands of stars over-head, even in the middle of a city. Stargazing was a universal pastime.

Today, most of us live in places where the stars are hidden by light pollution. Understanding a bit about light pollution can help us avoid the worst of it and offer us a more rewarding experience of the night sky.

Light pollution is excessive, misdirected or unwanted artificial light. There are three kinds of light pollution: stray light, glare, and sky glow.

Stray light and glare make it hard for our eyes to adapt to the dark. When you're stargazing, find a spot sheltered from nearby lights. Trees and buildings are great for blocking light. Our eyes take about 20 minutes to fully adapt to the dark. When they do, we can see many more stars. But when you're stargazing, avoid sources of white light. It "resets" your night vision. Soft red light does not.

Sky glow affects the whole sky, not just your eyes. Websites such as darksitefinder.com offer light pollution maps that can help you find darker skies near where you live.

Light-polluted skies versus natural dark skies

WHAT CAN I DO?

You can learn more about the effects of light pollution, and help scientists study the issue, by taking part in the Globe at Night community science campaign (www.globeatnight.org). The program helps people like you easily measure and submit observations of night sky brightness with a computer or smartphone. All you need to do is look for stars on a clear, moonless night. The project website will give you all the details about where in the sky to look and how to measure sky brightness.

Want to do even more? Check out the International Dark-Sky Association (www.darksky.org) to learn about causes of and solutions to light pollution, including simple things you and your family can do to help.

MEASURING THE BRIGHTNESS OF STARS

For thousands of years, astronomers and stargazers have classified stars by their brightness. Modern astronomers use a system originally developed by the ancient Greeks, who grouped stars by magnitude. They called the brightest stars in the sky "first-magnitude." Dimmer stars were grouped together; the dimmest stars visible to the human eye considered to be "of the sixth-magnitude." This subjective system was used by western astronomers for thousands of years.

With the development of photography and precise, objective measurements of star brightness, the system was refined. Rather than simply being classified as first- or second-magnitude, stars are now assigned a precise value of apparent brightness. For example, Polaris (the North Star) has a magnitude of 1.97.

While the system has been refined, the framework remains the same—the brighter an object is, the lower its magnitude. The brightest objects in the sky, including the sun, moon, Venus, Jupiter, and Sirius, have negative magnitudes.

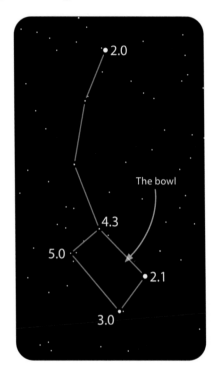

What Can I See?
You can rate how good the sky is for stargazing by determining your Limiting Visual Magnitude—the dimmest stars you can see in the sky. The stars of the Little Dipper offer a quick and convenient guide. The four stars that make up the bowl have magnitudes of about 2, 3, 4, and 5. If you can clearly see all four stars, you should be able to see every star on the charts in this book.

HELPFUL GEAR FOR STUDYING THE NIGHT SKY

Since you will spend most of your time looking up, it is nice to have a blanket and a pillow. Dress warmly. You won't be moving, and the night air can get surprisingly chilly, even in summer. You might want to bring a thermos with something warm to drink. In summer, bug spray doesn't hurt either!

It is helpful to have a red flashlight or headlamp. A red light will help you see without ruining your night vision. Flashlights and headlamps with a red LED built in are easy to find, and many are quite inexpensive. You can also make your own by securing a piece of translucent red plastic over a regular flashlight lens.

You don't need any equipment to study astronomy. Just your eyes. But binoculars and telescopes let you see even more. Binoculars are easier to use and are great for scanning the Milky Way and viewing craters on the moon. Quality telescopes can give amazing views, but they are expensive and require more skill to use. If you have one, take time to learn how to use it. Patience will pay off.

Unfortunately, most inexpensive telescopes are frustrating to use and offer disappointing views. If you are thinking of investing in a telescope, it's a good idea to try before you buy. One of the best ways to learn the basics of telescopes is to attend a star party put on by a local astronomy club, science museum, planetarium, or observatory. Check and see if there is one in your area.

Many amateur astronomers recommend a 4" to 6" Newtonian reflector as the best starter telescope. Orion and Meade are two of the most reputable manufactures of these kinds of telescopes.

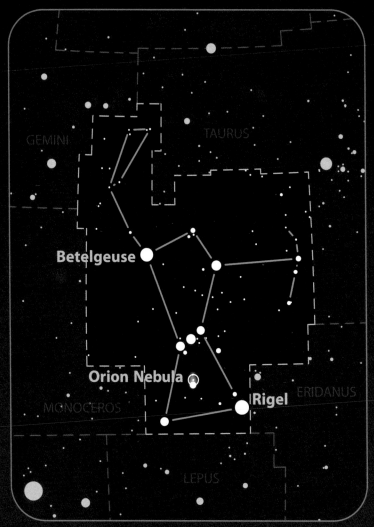

Orion is one of the 88 modern constellations. Green lines show the pattern of stars that help us recognize the constellation in the sky. The dashed line is the official border. Everything inside that line is considered to be part of the constellation Orion. Everything outside that line is part of a different constellation. Five other constellations share a border with Orion: Gemini, Taurus, Eridanus, Lepus, and Monoceros.

CONSTELLATIONS: MAPPING THE NIGHT SKY

The entire sky is too large to take in all at once. Since ancient times, people have identified patterns in the stars. Each pattern defines an area of the sky, which is called a constellation. Astronomers use constellations as a map of the sky. Every star in the sky is part of a constellation. The bright stars Betelgeuse and Rigel, for example, are in the constellation Orion. So is the famous star-forming nebula M42, which is also called the Orion Nebula.

What Can I See?

We can't see constellation boundaries. They are made up. We see stars. So every constellation in the sky is drawn around a recognizable pattern of stars. The Sky Tours (page 107) in this book will help you find and recognize many of these patterns.

How Do We Know?

Constellations are made up. Throughout history, different cultures have recognized different constellations. Peoples all over the world, for example, recognized the shape of a person with broad shoulders and a narrow waist in the stars of the modern constellation we call Orion. The Ancient Greeks associated these stars with the hero Orion from their mythology. Many Hindu people associated them with Kaalpurush, a representation of their god Vishnu. To the Navaho these stars represented the protector Atse Ats'oosi, usually translated as "First Slender One."

They marked the movement of these stars to time the planting and harvest of crops.

Modern astronomy grew out of the ancient Greek tradition. The ancient Greeks, in turn, were influenced by the Babylonian, Sumerian, and Egyptian cultures of early history. Drawing on this long history, the International Astronomical Union recognizes 88 official constellations. These constellations are used by professional and most amateur astronomers worldwide to map the sky.

Astronomical illustrations on the walls of a 2,000-year-old temple in Dendera, Egypt

THE CONSTELLATIONS OF THE ZODIAC

The path of the sun in the sky is called the ecliptic. The area of the sky that surrounds the ecliptic is called the zodiac. The moon and planets always appear along the zodiac, near the ecliptic. The ecliptic passes through thirteen constellations. Twelve of these constellations share their names with the astrological "houses of the zodiac."

What Can I See?

Look along the zodiac to spot the moon and planets. If you see a bright "star" near the ecliptic that doesn't appear on a star chart, it is probably a planet.

How Do We Know?

People have always taken a special interest in the path of the sun through the sky. Ancient Greek astronomers divided the area around the ecliptic into twelve equal segments they called "houses" and named each after a nearby constellation. They called these houses the zodiac, which means "circle of animals." Astronomers stopped using these houses centuries ago, but they continued using the constellations they were named after. Because of changes in the Earth's spin over time, today's constellations no longer line up with the ancient Greek zodiac. The dates the sun appears in each constellation are quite different from the traditional astrological dates. The chart on the next page shows the position of the sun throughout the year.

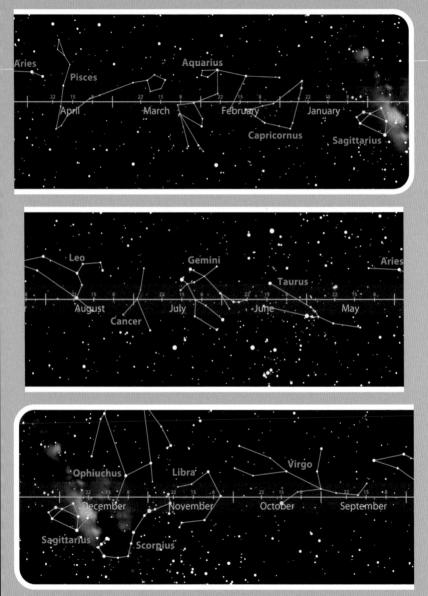

The zodiac chart; note that January starts on the top right.

You can use this chart to find the exact position of the sun on the day you were born and compare it to the ancient Greek zodiac dates shown below. As you can see, the dates are quite different than they were 2,000 years ago when the ancient Greeks used this.

Aries (see page 151)
Traditional: Mar 21–Apr 19
Apr 17–May 11

Taurus (see page 165)
Traditional: Apr 20–May 20
May 12–Jun 18

Gemini (see page 161)
Traditional: May 21–Jun 20
Jun 19–Jul 18

Cancer (see page 121)
Traditional: Jun 21–Jul 22
Jul 19–Aug 7

Leo (see page 119)
Traditional: Jul 23–Aug 22
Aug 8–Sep 14

Virgo (see page 117)
Traditional: Aug 23–Sep 22
Sep 15–Oct 28

Libra (see page 131)
Traditional: Sep 23–Oct 22
Oct 29–Nov 20

Scorpio (see page 131)
Traditional: Oct 23–Nov 21
Nov 21–Nov 28

Sagittarius (see page 135)
Traditional: Nov 22–Dec 21
Dec 16–Jan 17

Capricorn (see page 123)
Traditional: Dec 22–Jan 19
Jan 18–Feb 13

Aquarius (see page 151)
Traditional: Jan 20–Feb 18
Feb 14–Mar 9

Pisces (see page 151)
Traditional: Feb 19–Mar 20
Mar 10–Apr 16

Objects in the Night Sky

Some things we see in the night sky are small and close to the Earth. Others are unimaginably large and far away. It can be hard to tell the difference just by looking. It took astronomers thousands of years to figure out how far planets like Jupiter and Saturn are from the Earth. And it took hundreds of years after that to figure out how far away stars and galaxies are.

The constellation Orion, with the Orion Nebula, visible just below Orion's Belt; a photo of the nebula taken through a small telescope; and a high-resolution image taken through a larger telescope

Let's take a look at some of the things you can see in the night sky.

The moon: The largest and brightest object in the night sky.

Planets: The seven other bodies with their own, unique orbits around our sun.

Comets: Balls of ice and dust from the outer solar system that may occasionally come close enough to see from Earth.

Stars: Distant suns so far from Earth that they look like pinpoints of light in our sky.

Nebulae: Giant clouds of gas and dust, some of which are the birthplace of stars.

Star clusters: Collections of stars close together in space.

Galaxies: Enormous systems of billions of stars and other matter, bound together by gravity.

Meteors: Streaks of light caused by small pieces of space debris colliding with the Earth's atmosphere.

Venus passing in front of the sun

Our Solar System

Our solar system is the sun and all the objects bound to it by gravity. Only the sun shines with its own light. Other objects in our solar system reflect the light of our sun. Because they are so close to Earth, many appear bright in our sky. Objects in our solar system also appear to move against the "fixed" background stars.

Jupiter

Venus

The moon, Jupiter, and Venus reflecting the light of the setting sun

Earth compared
to the sun

The Sun

Diameter (in Earths):
109.298

Mass (in Earths): 330,000

The sun is our closest star, and the best-studied
star in the universe. As stars go, it is extremely
close—just 93 million miles from Earth (this distance
is known as one astronomical unit, or AU). That's
about 8 light minutes. The next closest star to Earth
is 4.4 light-years, or about 280,000 times as far.

What Can I See?
Don't look directly at the sun without protective
equipment. Always project its image or use a
specially designed solar filter. The Stanford Solar
Center (solar-center.stanford.edu) has a great web

page about safe ways to observe the sun. With simple equipment, you may be able to see dark areas called sunspots. The number of sunspots varies on a cycle of about 11 years. At the peak of the cycle, there may be dozens of sunspots visible at a time.

How Do We Know?

Since ancient times, some astronomers believed that the sun was much larger than the Earth and extremely far away. But making accurate measurements wasn't possible until the invention of the telescope. In 1672, astronomers Giovanni Cassini and Jean Richer used the apparent change of position, or parallax, of Mars to calculate the size of the solar system (see How Far Away Is the Sun? page 88). They showed that the sun was indeed many millions of miles from Earth.

In 1925, Cecilia Payne used spectroscopy (careful study of color in sunlight) to show that the sun was made mostly of hydrogen and helium (see What are Stars Made Of? page 97). Prior to her work, most scientists assumed the sun was made of rock and metal, like the Earth. Her discovery revolutionized our understanding of not only the sun, but of the entire universe.

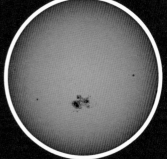

Sunspots (dark areas) visible on the sun

Compared to Earth

Orbit: 27.322 days

Distance from the Sun (in AU): 1

Diameter (in Earths): 0.273

Mass (in Earths): 0.012

1 AU = 93 million miles
(Earth's average distance from the sun)

The Moon

The moon is the brightest object in the night sky, our closest celestial neighbor, and the only natural object in orbit around the Earth. The full moon is about 30,000 times brighter than the brightest stars. The moon is much smaller than the sun, but it is also much closer to the Earth. By chance, the two appear the same size in our sky—roughly the size of your pinkie nail at arm's length.

Phases

The moon's most prominent feature is its sequence of phases. Half of the moon's surface is always lit,

but as the moon orbits the Earth we see different amounts of this lit surface.

When the moon is between the Earth and the sun, the side facing us is dark, making the moon invisible. This is called a "New Moon."

As the moon orbits the Earth, we begin to see it as a slender crescent in the evening sky growing larger, or "waxing," each night.

When the moon is a quarter of the way around the Earth, we see half of its disk illuminated. This "First Quarter" moon is visible in the evening sky and sets about midnight.

The moon continues to wax for another week becoming more round, or "gibbous," each night.

When the moon is on the opposite side of the Earth from the sun, we see it completely lit. The "Full Moon" is up all night, rising around sunset and setting close to sunrise.

As the moon enters the second half of its orbit, it "wanes," showing less of its lit surface each night. It rises about an hour later each evening, giving us a period of moonless sky after sunset.

The waning gibbous moon gives way to the "Third Quarter," then a waning crescent before disappearing from the sky on the next New Moon.

The full cycle of phases takes an average of 29½ days—about one month. In fact, the cycle of the moon is the origin of the month, and the moon's four quarters are the origin of the week.

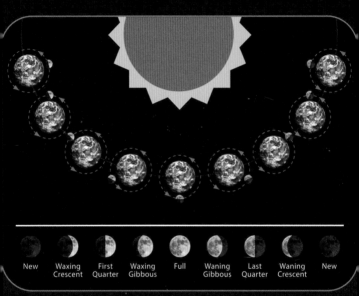

| New | Waxing Crescent | First Quarter | Waxing Gibbous | Full | Waning Gibbous | Last Quarter | Waning Crescent | New |

The Surface of the Moon

The face of the moon is a mosaic of light and dark regions. The dark regions, called *maria*, are the result of ancient lava flows. The moon is also covered with craters formed by asteroids striking its surface in the distant past. The moon rotates on its axis at the same rate it orbits the Earth. As a result, we always see the same face of the moon.

What Can I See?

With your naked eye, you can easily observe the moon's changing phases, see large maria, and spot a few of the most prominent craters. Binoculars will reveal many more. When using binoculars or a telescope, look near the "terminator," the line that marks the edge of sunlight. Here, the long shadows make lunar features easier to see.

How Do We Know?

Over 2,000 years ago, the Greek astronomer Aristarchus used parallax (see page 85) to measure the distance to the moon. When astronomers began using telescopes in the early 1600s, they discovered the moon's surface was covered with mountains, ridges, and craters. In 1753, the Serbo-Croatian scientist Roger Joseph Boscovich made careful observations of stars disappearing behind the moon and concluded that the moon did not have any atmo-

A lunar lander on the moon

sphere. Beginning in 1959, the Soviet Union and United States each sent a series of probes to the moon. The United States also launched a series of crewed space flights, called the Apollo missions, between 1969 and

1972. Twelve Apollo astronauts walked on the moon. They returned with samples of moon rocks that have helped scientists understand the origin of both the moon and the Earth. They also left instruments on the moon's surface to allow continued study.

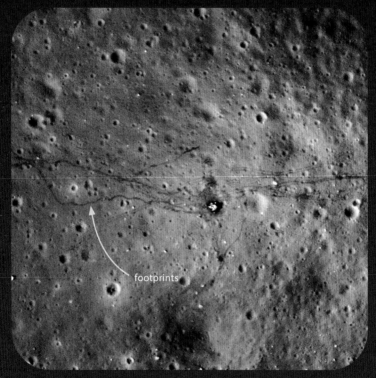

footprints

The Apollo 17 landing site viewed from space by the Lunar Reconnaissance Orbiter in 2011. The lines on this image are the footprints/tracks of the Apollo 17 astronauts, which are still preserved on the moon.

PLANETS

A planet is a large, round object that circles the sun in its own, unique orbit. There are eight known planets in our solar system, including the Earth. The five closest planets are among the brightest objects in the night sky.

To the naked eye, planets look like bright stars. But unlike stars, they change position in the sky from night to night. In fact, the word planet comes from the ancient Greek word for "wanderer."

Planets always appear close to the ecliptic—the apparent path of the sun across the sky. How a planet moves through the sky depends on the size of its orbit. Mercury and Venus have orbits smaller than the Earth's. They appear to cycle from one side of the sun to the other and are visible either in the west after sunset or in the east before sunrise. The other planets have orbits larger than Earth's and can appear anywhere along the ecliptic. The larger a planet's orbit, the longer it takes to circle the sun and the slower it appears to move against the background of "fixed" stars.

The planets of our solar system

Compared to Earth

Orbit: 88 days

Distance from the Sun (in AU): 0.39

Diameter (in Earths): 0.382

Mass (in Earths): 0.06

Mercury

Mercury is named for the Roman messenger of the gods, renowned for his swiftness. Mercury is the smallest planet in our solar system and the closest planet to the sun. It has a rocky surface, a metal core, and no atmosphere. Mercury's orbit and rotation are locked together in a curious way. If you were standing on the surface, Mercury would make one complete orbit around the sun between sunset and sunrise. A night on Mercury lasts an entire year!

First planet
from the sun

What Can I See?

Spotting Mercury is a rewarding challenge. Though bright, Mercury is always close to the sun and low in the sky during twilight, making it tricky to see. Binoculars help, but never look at the sun! Use an astronomy app or search online for the best times and places to look. Like the Moon, Mercury exhibits phases, which you can see in a good telescope.

How Do We Know?

The telescope was invented in 1609. Thirty years later, Italian astronomer Giovanni Zupi first recorded that Mercury has phases. This showed that Mercury orbits around the sun. Little else was known about the planet until the space age. Mercury has been visited by two spacecraft, *Mariner 10* and *MESSENGER*, which studied its structure and mapped the surface in great detail.

MESSENGER

Compared to Earth

Orbit: 225 days

Distance from the Sun (in AU): 0.72

Diameter (in Earths): 0.949

Mass (in Earths): 0.82

Venus

Venus is named for the Roman goddess of love and beauty. The planet is a dazzling namesake, shining brighter than anything else in the sky besides the sun and the moon. Venus has think clouds of carbon dioxide that trap heat from the sun. Its surface is hot enough to melt lead. But 30 miles up, above the clouds, the temperature is similar to Earth. Some scientists think humans could colonize Venus by building floating cloud cities.

Second planet from the sun

What Can I See?

Venus is hard to miss when it's high in the sky. Only the sun and moon shine brighter. As Venus orbits the sun, it cycles between our evening and morning skies. A complete cycle takes just over a year and a half. Venus shows phases, just like the moon. The phases are easy to see in a small telescope and may be visible to a sharp-eyed observer with binoculars.

The surface of Venus, taken by the *Venera 9* lander

How Do We Know?

Italian astronomer Galileo Galilei first observed the phases of Venus through a telescope in 1610. The phases showed that Venus orbits around the sun, not around the Earth. Modern telescopes allow scientists to study Venus's atmosphere. Twenty-six probes have visited Venus, including several landers. The landers have been short-lived, surviving only a few hours on the hot surface.

Compared to Earth

Orbit: 1.9 years (687 days)

Distance from the Sun (in AU): 1.52

Diameter (in Earths): 0.532

Mass (in Earths): 0.11

Mars

Mars gets its name from the Roman god of war, perhaps because of its red color. The color comes from iron oxide, or rust, on the surface. Mars is smaller than Earth and has a thin atmosphere and low gravity. Even so, some scientists and explorers would like to send people to Mars someday.

Fourth planet
from the sun

What Can I See?

Mars's distinctive red color makes it easy to identify. Most of the time, Mars is far from Earth and is
dimmer than many stars, so you need to know where
to look. Once every two years, Mars passes close to
Earth and can shine brighter than any star. Known as
oppositions, these are the best times to view the red
planet. Binoculars show a tiny disk. A telescope can
show details on the surface, including polar ice caps.

How Do We Know?

Telescope observations from the late 1800s showed
colors on the Martian surface changing with the
seasons. Many scientists believed this was evidence

of a growing season,
which would have
meant life on Mars.
By 1925, further
studies proved there
is not enough water
or oxygen on the
planet to support
complex life. Since
1960, Mars has been
the target of over
50 space missions,

Ingenuity, the helicopter that made the
first powered flight on another world

and there are currently about a dozen spacecraft
exploring the planet. Most are orbiters, but Mars is
also home to 3 rovers and a tiny helicopter.

Compared to Earth

Orbit: 11.9 years
Distance from the Sun (in AU): 5.2
Diameter (in Earths): 11.209
Mass (in Earths): 317.8

Jupiter

Jupiter is named for the king of the Roman gods. Jupiter is the largest planet and has more than twice the mass of all the other plants combined. Jupiter is made mostly of hydrogen and helium. It has a thick, turbulent atmosphere with colorful bands of clouds and powerful storms. Jupiter's Great Red Spot is a hurricane twice the size of the Earth that has been raging for more than 350 years.

Fifth planet
from the sun

What Can I See?

Jupiter is striking in the sky, shining brighter than any star. Binoculars can show Jupiter's four brightest moons: Io, Europa, Ganymede, and Callisto. The moons orbit quickly, offering a different view every night. A small telescope will show Jupiter's colorful cloud bands and the Great Red Spot.

How Do We Know?

In 364 BCE, Chinese astronomer Gan De (甘德) wrote a book about Jupiter. He didn't call it Jupiter, of course. He called it "*Sui Xing*." He recorded the movement of *Sui Xing* across the sky and described a small "companion," which may have been one of the planet's moons. Nearly 2,000 years later, in 1610, Italian astronomer Galileo Galilei turned one of the world's first telescopes to Jupiter and spotted four moons. As telescopes improved, astronomers discovered Jupiter's cloud bands and Great Red Spot. Two space probes, *Galileo* and *Juno*, orbited Jupiter for years, studying the planet and its moons. Seven other space probes have flown past Jupiter as part of longer missions.

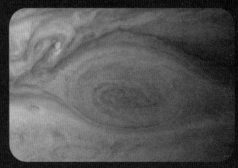

Jupiter's Great Red Spot

Compared to Earth

Orbit: 29.5 years

Distance from the Sun (in AU): 9.54

Diameter (in Earths): 9.449

Mass (in Earths): 95.2

Saturn

Saturn is named after the father of Jupiter in Roman mythology. It is nearly as large as Jupiter, but much farther away. Although large, Saturn has the lowest density of any planet. If you could build a bathtub large enough, Saturn would float. Saturn is most famous for its striking system of rings.

Sixth planet from the sun

What Can I See?

Saturn shines about as bright as the brightest stars in the sky. It has a distinctive yellowish color that makes it easy to pick out along the zodiac. Saturn is one of the most beautiful sights to view in a small telescope. A telescope of almost any size will show the planet's famous rings. Larger telescopes will show increasing detail and color.

Saturn's famous rings

How Do We Know?

Using his early telescopes, Galileo Galilei was the first to see that Saturn had an unusual shape. In 1659, with better telescopes, Dutch astronomer Christiaan Huygens first described the odd shape as a ring around the planet. He also discovered Saturn's largest moon, Titan. Three space probes flew past Saturn in the 1970s and '80s. In 1994, the *Cassini–Huygens* space probe arrived. It orbited Saturn for 13 years, studying the planet, its rings, and its moons. The probe revealed that some of Saturn's moons are more complex than previously thought and might even be able to support primitive life.

Orbit: 84 years
Distance from the Sun (in AU): 19.22
Diameter (in Earths): 4.007
Mass (in Earths): 14.6

Uranus

Uranus is named for the Greek god of the sky. Unknown to ancient cultures, it was the first planet discovered during recorded history. Uranus is the third-largest planet. It is about twice as far from the sun as Saturn. Uranus has a distinctive bluish-green color that comes from methane gas in its thick atmosphere.

Seventh planet from the sun

What Can I See?

Uranus is easy to see in binoculars. Under good, dark skies, it is even visible to the naked eye. But you need a good up-to-date star chart to know exactly where to look. In a telescope, Uranus appears faintly bluish-green. Above about 100x magnification, it looks like a tiny disk—which is how it was first discovered.

A crescent view of Uranus as seen from the *Voyager 2* space probe

How Do We Know?

When William Herschel spotted Uranus in 1781, he noticed that it looked like a tiny disk rather than a star. He watched it for several weeks to see if it moved against the other stars. When he saw that it did, he shared his observations with other astronomers. Together they concluded that it was a new planet beyond the orbit of Saturn. Uranus has been visited by one spacecraft, *Voyager 2*, which studied the planet's magnetic field, atmosphere, and weather.

Compared to Earth

Orbit: 164.8 years

Distance from the Sun (in AU): 30.06

Diameter (in Earths): 3.883

Mass (in Earths): 17.2

Neptune

Neptune is named for the Roman god of the sea. It has a bluish color, similar to Uranus, also caused by methane in its atmosphere. Neptune is the most distant planet from the sun, at least the most distant we know of. Neptune takes 165 years to orbit the sun. Only one "year" has passed on Neptune since it was first discovered. Neptune is also the windiest planet, with wind speeds up to 1,240 mph.

Eighth planet from the sun

What Can I See?

Neptune is the only known planet that is too dim to see with the naked eye. In a small telescope, Neptune looks like a small, bluish point of light. It is no brighter than most of the surrounding stars, so you need a detailed star chart to pick it out. Neptune is difficult to spot with binoculars.

How Do We Know?

Neptune was the first object in space to be predicted by math before it was discovered. Two mathematicians predicted that an unknown planet must be affecting the orbit of Uranus. Their predictions were confirmed by telescope observations in 1846. Most of what we know about Neptune comes from the *Voyager 2* spacecraft, which visited

A large cloud system on Neptune

Neptune in 1989, *Voyager 2* measured Neptune's rotation for the first time, measured the planet's mass, and studied its atmosphere and magnetic field.

ASTEROIDS, DWARF PLANETS, AND COMETS

Our solar system contains countless bodies that orbit around the sun but are too small to be considered planets. These objects are roughly divided into three groups: asteroids, dwarf planets, and comets.

ASTEROIDS

Asteroids are small, rocky objects that orbit around the sun. Most asteroids orbit in a band between Mars and Jupiter called the asteroid belt. Others are scattered about the inner solar system. There may be more than a million asteroids, but most are tiny. Only a few hundred are large enough to ever spot with a small or medium-sized telescope.

951 Gaspra, an asteroid, as seen from a robotic probe

What Can I See?

The brightest asteroids are visible in small telescopes and sometimes in binoculars. Unlike most planets, which look like tiny disks in a telescope, asteroids look like stars. In fact, the word "asteroid" means "star-like." You will need detailed star charts and information about each asteroid's current location to pick them out.

How Do We Know?

The first asteroid was discovered in 1801 by Italian astronomer Giuseppe Piazzi when he spotted what looked like a star moving compared to the other stars. At first, many astronomers thought this must be a new planet and named it Ceres. But Ceres was so small that it looked like a pinpoint of light,

Vespa, a large asteroid, seen from a visiting spacecraft

even in the largest telescopes. Over the next six years, three similar objects were discovered: Pallas, Juno, and Vesta. Astronomers realized that these were not planets after all, but a whole new group of objects. By 1891, 300 asteroids had been discovered. That year, astronomers began using photography to search for asteroids and discovered another 300 in just 15 years. Today, more than half a million asteroids have been identified.

DWARF PLANETS

Dwarf planets are round, like planets, but are smaller and share their orbits with other objects. The most famous dwarf planets

Ceres, a dwarf planet found in the asteroid belt, as seen from a robotic probe

are Ceres and Pluto. Both were considered planets when they were first discovered, but were reclassified after other, similar objects, such as Eris, were found. Ceres orbits between Mars and Jupiter and is also considered an asteroid. All the other dwarf planets are more distant than Neptune. Pluto is the exception, as it is sometimes closer to the sun than Neptune thanks to its odd orbit.

Pluto, the most famous dwarf planet, as seen by *New Horizons*

What Can I See?

Ceres is visible in binoculars or a small telescope. It looks like a point of light. Pluto is faintly visible in a large telescope, but it is difficult to spot.

How Do We Know?

In 1903, astronomer Percival Lowell predicted that a ninth planet was affecting the orbit of Neptune. He called his prediction "Planet X." In 1929, he built an observatory and hired a young assistant named Clyde Tombaugh to help search for it. Tombaugh took photographs every night, then studied them for objects that moved. After ten months

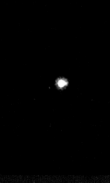

Eris, and its moon Dysnomia, as seen from the Hubble space telescope

of searching, Tombaugh discovered Pluto. It turned out that Lowell was mistaken and there was no Planet X. But in searching, Tombaugh discovered a whole new kind of object previously unknown to science. He also discovered a comet, 15 asteroids, and hundreds of variable stars. Most of what we know about Pluto today comes from the *New Horizons* space probe which flew past the dwarf planet in 2015.

COMETS

Comets are small chunks of ice and dust leftover from the formation of the solar system. Most comets exist in the distant solar system, beyond the orbit of Neptune. Some comets are thought to orbit as much as a light-year away from the sun. Occasionally, a comet will enter the inner solar system and be visible from Earth. When a comet gets close to the sun, it warms up and gives off gas and dust. This forms a cloud around the comet called a coma. Sometimes the gas and dust will stretch out in a long tail behind the comet. The dust left behind by some comets is the source of meteor showers on Earth. Most comets seen from Earth disappear back into the outer solar system. A few, such as the famous Halley's Comet, have smaller orbits and return every few decades.

What Can I See?

It is usually difficult to predict when a comet will be visible. You will usually need customized star charts to locate a comet. Astronomy magazines often include such charts. It is rare for any comet to get bright enough to be seen with the naked eye. Most years, there are one or more comets bright enough to spot in binoculars and a few bright enough to see in a small telescope. They typically look like tiny, fuzzy spots of light.

How Do We Know?

People have recorded observations of comets since ancient times. Some ancient astronomers believed they were a kind of cloud in the atmosphere. Others believed they existed out among the stars. In 1577, astronomers Tycho Brahe and Michael Maestlin made parallax measurements (see page 85) of a comet and found that it was farther away than the moon. In 1687, the physicist Isaac Newton used mathematical patterns to show that comets orbit the sun. Then in 1705, Edmond Halley used Newton's method to predict the return of a comet in 1759—the first successful prediction of a comet in human history.

Halley's Comet in 1986

STARS

Stars look like pinpoints of light, sparkling in the night. Though they appear tiny, stars are actually distant suns, similar to our own. Each is an enormous ball of super-hot gas glowing from the heat of nuclear fusion. Fusion means "to join," and during nuclear fusion elements (such as hydrogen) are compressed together, which creates new elements (such as helium). This process also releases a great deal of heat and light. No one knows how many stars there are, but the number must be unimaginably large. Astronomers estimate that there are about 200 billion stars in our galaxy alone.

What Can I See?

How many stars we can see depends on how dark the sky is. Under the clearest, darkest sky, you may be able to see about 4,000 stars spread across the sky. Light pollution, haze, or the light of the moon will all reduce that number. In a typical rural area, you might be able to see 3,000 stars. In the suburbs, you might be able to pick out 1,000. In urban areas, there are often fewer than 100 stars visible. Wherever

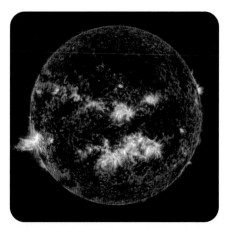

The best-studied star in the universe: our sun

you are, binoculars or a small telescope will allow you to see many more stars.

The Hyades cluster in the constellation Taurus has a mix of hot (blue) and cooler (orange) stars.

How Do We Know?

Little was known about stars until the modern age. Since ancient times, astronomers have tried to figure out how far away the stars are. The distance is so difficult to measure that no one succeeded until 1838 (see How Far Away Are the Stars? page 90). It took almost another century for scientists to figure out that stars are balls of gas lit by nuclear fusion (see What Are Stars Made Of? page 97).

DOUBLE STARS

Sometimes what looks like one star is actually two. Stars that appear close together in the sky are called double stars. Some double stars are optical doubles—stars that appear close together, but are different distances from Earth. Others are multi-star systems, bound together by gravity. These are called binary stars.

What Can I See?

Some double stars are far enough apart to spot with your naked eye. A few of these, such as the famous pair of Mizar and Alcor in the handle of the Big Dipper, are true binary systems.

Other double stars can be split using binoculars or a telescope. In 1617, using the newly invented telescope, the Italian astronomer Benedetto Castelli discovered that Mizar itself was a double star. The two stars are now called Mizar A and Mizar B and can be easily seen in binoculars.

How Do We Know?

Most binary stars are so close together that they look like a single point of light, even in the largest telescopes. But the light of each star has a distinctive pattern of colors, called a spectrum. In the late 1800s, the astronomer Antonia

Antonia Maury

Maury did groundbreaking work in the new science of stellar spectroscopy (the careful study of colors in starlight). Her research team discovered that Mizar A is in fact two stars, each with its own spectrum. Such stars are now called spectroscopic binaries. Maury went on to develop the modern system for classifying stars, based on their spectra.

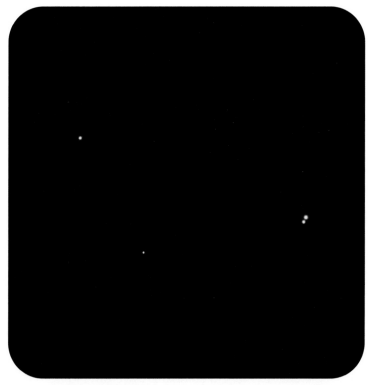

The Mizar and Alcor star system as it appears in a telescope. The system has at least six stars. Some can be seen naked eye, others with binoculars, and some only through spectroscopy.

VARIABLE STARS

Most stars in the sky appear to shine with a steady light. But some stars brighten and dim over time. Astronomers call these variable stars. There are many kinds of variable stars. Some brighten and dim on a predictable schedule. Others are irregular. Some, like Cepheid variables, actually grow and shrink over time. Others, like the eclipsing binary Algol, change because some of their light gets blocked from our view.

What Can I See?

Some variable stars are bright enough to track with your naked eyes. These include Algol (see Perseus, Fall Tour, page 149), Betelgeuse (see Orion, Winter Tour, page 155), Delta Cephei (see Cassiopeia and Cepheus, Fall Tour, page 143), and Sheliak (see Lyra, Summer Tour, page 129). The changes are subtle. You will need to pay careful attention to notice them. Compare each star to other bright stars around them to follow their cycles of brightening and dimming.

How Do We Know?

Ancient astronomers noticed that some stars would occasionally brighten or dim, but there are no detailed records from ancient times. The time it takes for a variable star to make a complete cycle of brightening and dimming is called its period. It wasn't until 1638 that Johannes Holwards first recorded the period of a variable star—the 11-month cycle of the star Mira. Thirty years later, Geminiano Montanari published a description of Algol's 2 day, 21 hour-long period. In

1784, John Goodricke suggested that Algol might be an eclipsing binary star. His suspicion was confirmed a century later, in 1889, after the invention of spectroscopy (see page 60).

Astronomers study variable stars by plotting their brightness over time. These plots are called light curves. By looking for patterns in these light curves, astronomers learn about these stars. Many amateur astronomers make regular measurements of variable stars and contribute to this research as members of the American Association of Variable Star Observers (www.aavso.org). Perhaps you will be one of them. Anyone can join.

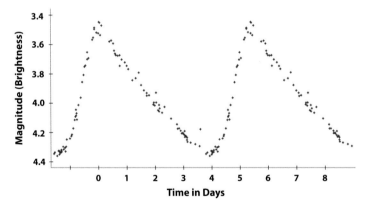

The light curve of Delta Cephei shows the distinctive "shark fin" shape of all Cepheid variables. Cepheids pulsate, growing and shrinking in size over the course of a few days. Edwin Hubble used patterns in the light curves of Cepheid variables to measure the distance to the Andromeda Galaxy (see How Far Away Are Other Galaxies, page 92)

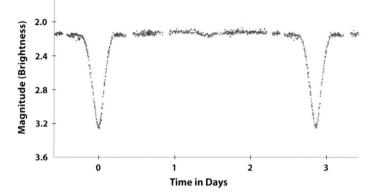

The light curve of the eclipsing binary star system Algol. The sharp dips occur when the dimmer star in the system passes in front of the brighter one, blocking much of its light. These dips occur every 2 days, 20 hours, and 49 minutes. The tiny dip in the middle of the chart occurs when the brighter star passes in front of the dimmer one. This dip can only be measured with sensitive cameras. Astronomers look for even smaller dips than this to detect possible exoplanets around distant stars.

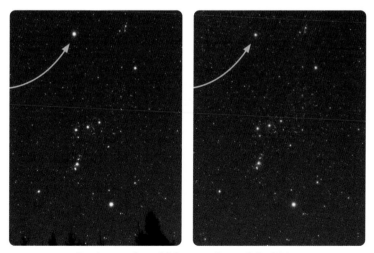

Betelgeuse, the reddish star to the top left of Orion, is a variable star. The photo on the left is from 2012; the one on the right is from 2022, when it was much dimmer.

EXOPLANETS

A planet outside of our solar system is called an exoplanet. Exoplanets are too small and too far away to see with the unaided eye. But by using clever techniques and careful measurements, scientists have discovered thousands of exoplanets orbiting around distant stars.

The first exoplanet to be directly photographed, 2M1207b, is seen orbiting its host star about 230 light-years from Earth. The planet is about five times the size of Jupiter.

How Do We Know?

Most exoplanets are discovered by recording planetary transits. A transit is when one object passes in front of another. If an exoplanet lines up just right, it blocks a tiny amount of the light we see each time it orbits its star. Sensitive instruments, such as the *Gaia* space telescope, can detect these regular dips in starlight.

What Can I See?

The drop in starlight from a planetary transit is too small to see with your eyes. But there are transits you can observe. Algol is a special kind of variable star in the constellation Perseus (see Fall Tour page 139) called a transiting binary. Approximately every three days, the stars pass in front of one another. By comparing Algol's brightness to other nearby stars, you can see this dimming for yourself. A few times each century, we can see a planet transit our own star. Mercury will transit the sun in 2032, 2039, 2049, and 2052. The transit of 2049 will be visible from the United States.

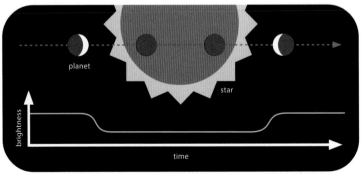

Light curve of a transiting planet

The Ring Nebula (M57)

DEEP SKY OBJECTS

Deep sky objects are objects larger than individual stars that exist beyond our solar system. These include nebulae (clouds of gas and dust), clusters of stars, and other galaxies.

The Whirlpool Galaxy (M51) through a telescope

What Can I See?

Most deep sky objects are very faint and can only be seen with a telescope. A handful are visible with the naked eye under clear, dark skies. Most look like soft, fuzzy patches of light. Larger telescopes will show greater structure and detail.

How Do We Know?

In 1758, a French astronomer named Charles Messier began searching for the comet predicted by Edmond Halley (see Comets, page 56). While searching, Messier spotted the Crab Nebula and mistook it for a comet. His mistake motivated him to create a list of objects to ignore while searching for comets. The list grew to 110 entries and became the first catalog of deep sky objects. Objects in the Messier Catalog are listed with an M (for Messier) followed by a number. The Crab Nebula is M1. Later astronomers, using larger telescopes, created much larger catalogs of deep sky objects—but to this day, most astronomers use Messier's original catalog numbers when they can.

NEBULAE

A nebula is a giant clouds of gas and dust in space. From Earth, they look like soft, fuzzy patches in the night sky. Some of these giant clouds are the birth-places of stars. Others are the ghostly shells of stars that have died.

What Can I See?

M42, the Orion Nebula, is visible to the naked eye as a soft patch of light near the tip of the "sword" in Orion (Winter Tour). It is one of the best-studied star-forming regions in the sky. Binoculars show some shape and structure, while a small telescope reveals beautiful texture and many young stars.

M1, the Crab Nebula, is the remains of a supernova, an exploding star, in the constellation Taurus (Winter Tour page 153). It is too faint to see with the naked eye, but it is visible in binoculars as a small, faint blotch of light. A good telescope will show strands extending out from the center.

The Orion Nebula (M42) through a telescope

How Do We Know?

In 1054, Chinese astronomers recorded a "Guest Star" in the constellation Taurus. This star was so bright that it was visible during the day for three weeks before fading. Centuries later, astronomers learned that the largest stars in the galaxy explode at the end of their lives. These massive explosions are called supernovas. In the 1920s, astronomers noticed that the Crab Nebula was expanding. Based on its speed of expansion, they calculated that it could be the result of a star exploding about 900 years earlier. By 1942, astronomers concluded that the Crab Nebula was the remnant of the "Guest Star" recorded by Chinese scholars in 1054.

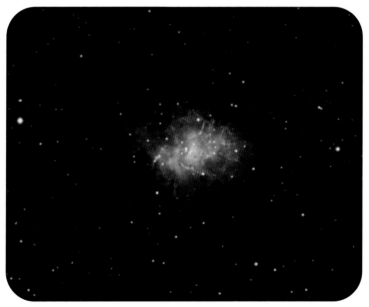

The Crab Nebula (M1)

STAR CLUSTERS

Star clusters are large groups of stars that move through space together. There are two kinds of star clusters: open clusters and globular clusters.

Open clusters are groups of younger stars that formed at the same time and are still close together.

What Can I See?

The Pleiades (M45) in the constellation Taurus (Winter Tour page 153) is the most famous star cluster in the sky. It is easy to see with the naked eye and spectacular in binoculars.

The Praesepe (M44) through a small telescope

The Praesepe (M44) in the constellation Cancer (Spring Tour page 107) is visible on clear nights as a faint, fuzzy circle about three times the diameter of the full moon. Binoculars reveal a dense bunching of stars.

The Double cluster in the constellation Perseus (Fall Tour page 139) is just visible to the naked eye under clear, dark skies.

Globular clusters are huge, ancient groups of stars that orbit our galaxy's core. Globular clusters can contain hundreds of thousands of stars. Most are extremely far away and difficult to see without a telescope.

What Can I See?

M13 is a globular cluster in the constellation Hercules (Summer Tour page 123). To the naked eye, it looks like a faint, fuzzy star. It is one of the most popular objects to view with a small telescope.

M13 through a small telescope

How Do We Know?

The Praesepe was one of the first things that Galileo observed with the newly invented telescope in 1609. He discovered that it was not a nebula, as had been thought, but a dense cluster of stars. His discovery that there were many more stars than the eye alone could see helped pave the way for the scientific revolution of the seventeenth century.

The Andromeda Galaxy (M31)

GALAXIES

Galaxies are enormous collections of stars, gas, and dust, separated from each other by vast areas of relatively empty space. Galaxies come in many shapes and sizes. They can contain anywhere from a few million to over a trillion stars. Our solar system is part of a galaxy we call the Milky Way. The universe contains hundreds of billions of galaxies. A few are visible with the naked eye. Many more are visible in binoculars and small telescopes.

What Can I See?

The Milky Way is made up of some 200 billion stars. Their collective light blends together in a band that stretches across our sky. Beautiful under clear, dark skies, the rich star fields of the Milky Way are great places to scan with binoculars.

M31, the Andromeda Galaxy (Fall Tour page 139) is visible to the naked eye as a faint, fuzzy oval. At 2.5 million light-years from Earth, it is the most distant object visible without optical aid.

Like most galaxies, M51, The Whirlpool Galaxy (Spring Tour page 107), is too faint to see with the naked eye, but it is dazzling in a small telescope.

How Do We Know?

Until the 1920s, no one knew there were any galaxies beyond the Milky Way. An object like M31 was called a "spiral nebula" and was thought to be part of our galaxy. In 1924, the astronomer Edwin Hubble used the new method of standard candles (see How Far Away Are Other Galaxies? page 92) to measure the distance to M31. His measurements proved that M31 was much too distant to be part of the Milky Way and must be a whole galaxy unto itself. The universe was larger than anyone had ever imagined.

The Whirlpool Galaxy (M51)

CLOSER TO HOME

Some of what we see in the night sky is quite close to home. Auroras and meteors come from material entering Earth's atmosphere from outer space. Artificial satellites and airplanes sometimes resemble stars at first glance.

MANMADE OBJECTS

Thousands of satellites and spacecraft orbit the Earth. Though small, they are quite close, and some shine brightly when lit by the sun. In fact, when sun glints off the large solar panels of the International Space Station, it can outshine the brightest stars and planets. Many other satellites can be seen as faint points of light that drift across the sky. Some websites

The International Space Station over northern Minnesota

and mobile apps give predictions for the best time to spot satellites. The most popular site is Heavens Above (www.heavens-above.com).

Some high-flying aircraft might look like a star or planet at first. But they move too slowly to be a meteor, and too fast to be a star or planet. Also, many aircraft have blinking lights.

A sweeping display of the northern lights (auroras)

AURORAS

Auroras are colorful light shows in the night sky, caused by the sun. Auroras happen when charged particles from the sun interact with gases in the Earth's atmosphere. This can produce anything from a faint glow in the sky to vivid sheets of iridescent colors streaming down from above. The charged particles are funneled by the Earth's magnetic field, so auroras are usually seen near the Earth's north and south magnetic poles. The number of charged particles sent by the sun changes. Sometimes, the sun sends out huge numbers of particles at once. These "solar storms" cause the strongest auroras. Auroras near the north pole are often called the northern lights; those near the south pole are known as the southern lights.

How Do We Know?

In the mid-1700s, scientists began to notice a link between auroras and electrical and magnetic activity. In the early 1900s, a Norwegian scientist named Kristian Birkeland wrote a book suggesting how auroras form. Birkeland spent years studying electricity, magnetism, auroras, and solar activity. He came up with patterns that he thought could explain the aurora—but there was no way to test his ideas from the ground. In 1967, measurements from a weather satellite proved that Birkeland was correct.

What Can I See?
The northern lights are most common near the north pole and become dimmer and less common the farther south you go. It is extremely rare to see the northern lights in the southern half of the United States.

METEOR SHOWERS
Meteors, poetically called "shooting stars," are small pieces of rock, ice, dust, and other space debris burning up in Earth's atmosphere.

What Can I See?
Meteors may be seen at any time. Most nights, there may be a few dozen meteors bright enough to see under clear, dark skies. Several times each year, the Earth passes through a cloud of debris, and dozens of meteors may be visible every hour. These events are called meteor showers.

How Do We Know?
Meteors have been observed and recorded throughout human history, but their nature was a mystery until the nineteenth century. In November of 1833, an unusually strong meteor shower brought thousands of

meteors every hour. Careful observers noticed that all the meteors seemed to radiate from the same point in the sky. Astronomers studied first-hand reports from across the United States and concluded that

A meteor in the Perseid meteor shower

the meteors originated beyond the Earth. They correctly predicted that another strong meteor shower would take place around the same dates in 1866. Shortly after this, the Italian astronomer Giovanni Schiaparelli linked the showers to the orbit of the comet Tempel-Tuttle and proposed that meteors were material from the tails of comets striking the Earth's atmosphere.

Astronomers still rely on observations by the general public to learn about meteors. To learn how you can contribute, visit the American Meteor Society (www.amsmeteors.org). They even have an App for iPhones and Androids to help you observe and report meteors.

Major Meteor Showers	From	To	Peak
Quadrantids	Jan 1	Jan 10	Jan 4
Eta Aquariids	Apr 19	May 26	May 7
Perseids	Jul 13	Aug 26	Aug 12
Geminids	Dec 4	Dec 16	Dec 14

How Do We Know?

Astronomers use science to learn about the universe. Science is the careful, first-hand study of nature. Scientists build on previous knowledge by asking questions, making observations, looking for patterns, and sharing with others. Here is how one ancient scientist measured the size of the Earth, more than 2,200 years ago.

Eratosthenes was a scientist who lived from 276 to 195 BCE. He was in charge of the Library of Alexandria, which was the largest and most complete collection of human knowledge in the ancient world.

Building on previous knowledge and asking questions

In his book *On the Heavens*, the Greek philosopher Aristotle explained how we can know the Earth is a sphere. Eratosthenes read Aristotle's work, and he knew the Earth was round. What he wanted to find out was how big it was.

ARISTOTLE OFFERED THREE POINTS:

1. Every portion of the Earth tends toward the center until by compression and convergence they form a sphere.

2. Travelers going south see southern constellations rise higher above the horizon.

3. The shadow of Earth on the moon during a lunar eclipse is round.

Making observations

From his reading, Eratosthenes knew that the sun was directly overhead on the first day of summer in the city of Syene, Egypt. In Alexandria, the sun was never directly overhead. On the first day of summer, Eratosthenes measured shadows cast by flagpoles in the city.

Looking for patterns

Using geometry, Eratosthenes calculated the angle of the sun in Alexandria to be 1/50th of a complete circle. That meant that the distance around the Earth must be 50 times the distance from Syene to Alexandria. Syene is about 520 miles south of Alexandria. Using these numbers, Eratosthenes calculated a size for the Earth that is quite close to our modern measurement of 24,900 miles.

Sharing with others

Eratosthenes recorded his observations and calculations in books, which he added to the Library of Alexandria. This allowed later scientists to build on his work. His original books were lost, but later scholars referred to his work.

TOOLS OF ASTRONOMY

Science advances when scientists make new or better measurements. New tools let scientists measure new things or measure things more accurately.

Telescopes allow astronomers to see dimmer objects. They also magnify what we see, allowing more precise measurements. Telescopes revolutionized astronomy. As telescopes have improved, so has our understanding of the universe.

The telescope William Herschel used to discover the planet Uranus

What looks like plain, white light to our eyes is made up of many different colors mixed together. Prisms separate light into its component colors. This is called a spectrum. A rainbow is an example of a spectrum. Raindrops act as prisms to separate sunlight into its component colors. Different materials give off, absorb, or reflect different colors of light. Materials also absorb or give off light differently at different temperatures. By studying spectra, scientists can learn what stars are made of.

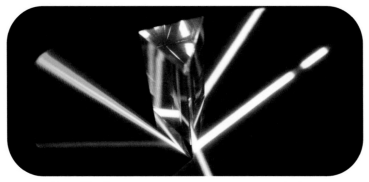

Prisms like this one separate light into its component colors.

Photographs capture images allowing us to compare scenes over time and look for patterns that are hard to see with our eyes alone.

January 23, 1930

January 29, 1930

Clyde Tombaugh discovered the dwarf planet Pluto in 1930 by comparing photographs side by side. Pluto is the tiny dot pointed out by the arrows

Hubble shown in Earth orbit

Since it was lunched in 1990, the Hubble Space Telescope has use spectral filters and digital cameras to make more than 1.5 million astronomical observations.

The Hubble Deep Field: the deepest-ever look at the early universe.
Every object in this photograph is an entire galaxy.

HOW FAR AWAY ARE CELESTIAL OBJECTS?

When we look at the night sky, everything seems to be the same distance away. We can't tell just by looking if some stars are closer than others. If we pay close attention, we can occasionally see stars disappear behind the moon—so we know the moon is closer than the stars. But how much closer?

Long ago, astronomers figured out that they could use parallax to measure distances to objects in the night sky.

Parallax is the change we see in the apparent position of an object when we shift our point of view. As we move, objects that are close appear to change position more than objects that are far away. You can see this

Parallax is easy to observe from a car.

for yourself the next time you are riding in a car. When you look out the window, objects close to the road will appear to zip by quickly, while objects that are far away will seem to pass by more slowly.

Another way to see parallax is to hold one finger out in front of your face. Then close one eye at a time. Your finger will appear to move back and forth against the background.

The same thing happens when people look at the sky from two different places on Earth. Objects closer to the Earth will appear to move more than objects that are farther away.

HOW FAR AWAY IS THE MOON?

The Greek astronomer Aristarchus, who lived from 310 to 230 BCE, used parallax to measure the distance to the moon. Aristarchus made careful measurements of the Earth's shadow on the moon during a lunar eclipse. He used geometry to calculate the distance to the moon as about 57 times the radius of the Earth. The radius is the distance from the center of a ball to its surface.

Today, astronomers measure the distance to the moon with lasers. These measurements are accurate to less than a millimeter. We now know that the distance to the moon changes as it orbits the Earth. But the average distance to the moon is just over 60 times the radius of the Earth. This is remarkably close to the measurement

Aristarchus made more than 2,200 years ago using only his naked eyes—and lots of smarts.

Aristarchus also tried to measure the distance to the sun. His measurements weren't very accurate, but they showed that the sun is much farther away than the moon, and therefore much larger. It would be 1,900 years before astronomers were able to measure the distance to the sun.

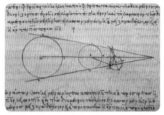

A copy of Aristarchus's work, showing his calculations of the distance to the moon

A partial lunar eclipse

HOW FAR AWAY IS THE SUN?

In the early 1600s, a German astronomer named Johannes Kepler discovered a mathematical pattern that described the movement of the planets. There were two parts to this pattern.

- Planets move in ellipses (oval-like shapes) with the sun as one focus
- A line connecting a planet to the sun sweeps out equal area in equal time.
- This means that the size of a planet's orbit is mathematically related to its period.

    (Here is the mathematical relationship, if you are curious: the square of the orbital period is proportional to the cube of the semi-major axis of the orbit.)

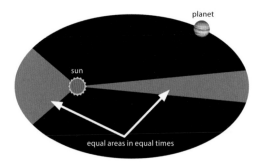

equal areas in equal times

Using this pattern, Kepler could calculate the size of each planet's orbit relative to the Earth by comparing the time it took for them to orbit the sun. Since Mercury, for example, orbits the sun in 88 days, it should orbit at 0.39 times (39%) the distance that the Earth does. Jupiter, which takes just under 12 years to circle the sun, orbits 5.2 times farther than the Earth.

The distance from the Earth to the sun became known as an astronomical unit (abbreviated AU). And the orbit of every planet could be calculated in AU. The problem was, nobody knew how large an astronomical unit was. If astronomers could measure the distance to any other planet, they could calculate the astronomical unit and measure the entire solar system.

In 1672, the Italian astronomer Giovanni Cassini used parallax to measure the distance to Mars. He drew the position of Mars against the background stars. His colleague, Jean Richer, traveled to French Guiana in South America and did the same. Cassini compared their drawings and used the distance between Paris and French Guiana to calculate the distance to Mars. From this, he calculated the distance from the Earth to the sun: 87 million miles

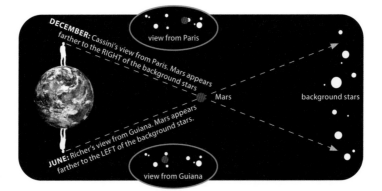

DECEMBER: Cassini's view from Paris. Mars appears farther to the RIGHT of the background stars

view from Paris

Mars

background stars

JUNE: Richer's view from Guiana. Mars appears farther to the LEFT of the background stars.

view from Guiana

As telescopes improved, astronomers used the parallax of other planets and asteroids to make better and better measurements of the astronomical unit. Over time, they arrived at a measurement of 93 million miles—a little more than what Cassini calculated. They also figured out how to use parallax to measure the distance to the stars.

Today, astronomers use radar to measure the distance to the sun with great accuracy.

HOW FAR AWAY ARE THE STARS?

Even the closest stars are incredibly far away. Their parallax is so small that for centuries most astronomers believed it was impossible to measure. It turns out that it is possible—just difficult. Even with the best measurements, the Earth isn't big enough to measure the parallax of a star. Astronomers need to use the Earth's orbit around the sun.

Over six months, the Earth will travel from one side of the sun to the other—a distance of two astronomical units. These two points of view are far enough apart to measure parallax for nearby stars.

The German astronomer Friedrich Bessel was the first person to measure the distance to a star. His research team spent 20 years carefully measuring the positions of 50,000 stars. From all these observations, Bessel was able to measure the parallax of a single star, called 61 Cygni, in the constellation Cygnus (see Summer tour, page 123). He announced his team's findings in 1838.

Bessel calculated that 61 Cygni was 660,000 astronomical units from Earth. This distance is so vast that Bessel noted it would take light more than ten years to travel that far. Soon after, astronomers began using light-years as a unit of measurement. A light-year is the distance that light travels in one Earth year. It is about 63,000 astronomical units or nearly 6 trillion miles.

Today, astronomers use data from the *Gaia* space telescope to calculate the distance to nearby stars. *Gaia* could measure the width of a human hair more than 500 miles away. But even *Gaia* can only measure distances up to about 30,000 light-years. Galaxies are much, much farther than that.

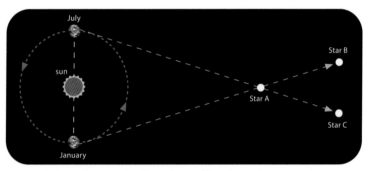

A simple example of how the parallax of a star is measured

The Andromeda Galaxy (M31)

HOW FAR AWAY ARE OTHER GALAXIES?

Any source of light, whether it's a porch light or a distant star, looks dimmer the farther you get from it. A 100-watt light bulb looks bright when it is at arm's length, but dim when seen from blocks away.

The amount of light an object gives off is called its luminosity. If you know an object's luminosity, you can figure out how far away it is by measuring how bright it appears. Objects with a known luminosity are called standard candles. But how do we know how much light a star gives off? Unlike a light bulb, we can't just look at the package.

In 1912, Henrietta Swan Leavitt discovered the first standard candle in astronomy. Leavitt worked at the Harvard Observatory where she studied variable stars.

She discovered a pattern in the light curves of stars called Cepheid variables: More-luminous Cepheid variables have longer periods. Put another way, the more light a Cepheid variable gives off, the slower it cycles between bright-

A Hubble Space Telescope image of RS Puppis, one of the Cepheid variables that Henrietta Swan Leavitt studied

ening and dimming. Her discovery made it possible for astronomers to calculate the luminosity of a Cepheid variable by measuring its period. And once astronomers know a star's luminosity, they can calculate how far away it is by measuring how bright it appears.

In 1924, Edwin Hubble used Leavitt's method to measure Cepheid variables in the Andromeda Galaxy (M31) and concluded that it must be more than 1 million light-years away. Later measurements with more-sensitive equipment revised that estimate to 2.5 million light-years.

In the following century, astronomers have identified other standard candles. Some are so bright that they are visible from billions of light-years away.

WHAT IS THE MASS OF THE EARTH?

Scientists have known the size of the Earth since Eratosthenes calculated it in the third century BCE (see How Do We Know? page 80). If we guess that the Earth is made of rock, we can estimate its mass. The density of solid rock is about three times that of water. Density is often measured in thousands of kilograms per cubic meter. A thousand kilograms is the mass of a small car. A cubic meter is the size of a large coffee table. So think about a small car crushed down to the size of a large coffee table. That's the density of water. The density of rock is about three times that, or 3,000 kilograms per cubic meter. If we multiply this by Eratosthenes' size of the Earth, we get a mass of three trillion-trillion kilograms. But is that right? Is the Earth solid rock?

In 1687, the English scientist Isaac Newton published his famous Law of Universal Gravitation. Newton believed that the same patterns that explained how objects fall on Earth could also explain how planets orbit the sun. This law stated:

· Every object is attracted to every other object by the force of gravity
· The force is proportional to the mass of the objects (more massive objects exert more force)
· The force drops off as the distance between objects increases (this distance is measured from the center of each object)

Newton's "law" accurately predicted the way objects fell to Earth. It explained the elliptical orbits of planets that Johannes Kepler described a few decades earlier (see How Far Away Is the Sun? page 88) It also predicted that the mass of the Earth is proportional to the weight of any object on its surface. Newton called the proportion in his law the gravitational constant. But in 1687, no one knew the value of the gravitational constant. Measuring it is really, really tricky, and it took 111 years for someone to do it.

In 1798, Henry Cavendish successfully measured the gravitational constant and calculated that the Earth was six trillion-trillion kilograms. That's twice as much as solid rock! That means the Earth's interior must be much denser. The Earth's core must be made of metal.

Finding the mass of other planets is trickier. We can make pretty good estimates from Earth using lots of careful measurement and a bit of guesswork, but the best measurements come from space probes "weighing" themselves as they fly past.

Using a planet's mass, scientists can make good, educated guesses about what each planet is made of. Mercury, Venus, Earth, and Mars are heavy for their size and must be made of dense materials like rock and metal. Jupiter, Saturn, Uranus, and Neptune are light for their size. They are made of less dense materials, like thick gases.

WHY KILOGRAMS INSTEAD OF POUNDS?

Weight is a measurement of force—it is the pressure you feel on the bottom of your feet when you stand. Mass is how much matter is in an object. Pounds are a measure of weight. Kilograms are a measure of mass. On Earth, one kilogram weighs 2.2 pounds. But on the moon, one kilogram weighs just under six ounces.

Neil Armstrong, the first person to set foot on the moon, had a mass of 77 kilograms. On Earth, he weighed 170 pounds. On the moon, he still had a mass of 77 kilograms, but he weighed just 28 pounds. Even with his massive space suit (about another 80 kilograms), he weighed only 60 pounds and could easily bound across the lunar surface.

Neil Armstrong on the surface of the moon

Planet/Moon	Mass (kg)	Weight (lbs.)
Earth	22.7 / 31.8 / 45.5	50 / 70 / 100
Moon	22.7 / 31.8 / 45.5	8.3 / 12 / 17
Mercury	22.7 / 31.8 / 45.5	19 / 27 / 38
Venus	22.7 / 31.8 / 45.5	45 / 63 / 90
Mars	22.7 / 31.8 / 45.5	19 / 27 / 38
Jupiter	22.7 / 31.8 / 45.5	126 / 177 / 253
Saturn	22.7 / 31.8 / 45.5	53 / 75 / 107
Uranus	22.7 / 31.8 / 45.5	44 / 62 / 89
Neptune	22.7 / 31.8 / 45.5	57 / 80 / 114
Pluto	22.7 / 31.8 / 45.5	3.2 / 4.4 / 6.3

WHAT ARE STARS MADE OF?

Early astronomers could only guess about the nature of the sun and stars. Most assumed that stars were made of the same materials as the Earth—mostly rocks and metal. That began to change in 1925, thanks to the work of Cecilia Payne.

As a graduate student at Harvard University, Cecilia Payne wrote her PhD thesis on the spectra of stars. A spectrum is the rainbow of colors visible after light has passed through a prism.

By applying new ideas, Payne came to two conclusions. First, she showed that most of the differences in the spectra of different stars was because of their temperature. Stars are mostly made of the same elements, just glowing at different temperatures. Hotter stars shine more blue, cooler stars shine more red. Second, she concluded that stars were made almost entirely of hydrogen.

Payne's discovery led British physicist Arthur Eddington to first suggest that stars are lit by the nuclear fusion of hydrogen into helium in their cores.

The distinguished astronomer Otto Struve described Payne's work as "the most brilliant PhD thesis ever written in astronomy."

Dr. Cecilia Payne discovered that stars are made mostly of hydrogen.

HOW FAST DOES LIGHT TRAVEL?

In 1672, a young Danish astronomer named Ole Rømer started working at the Paris Observatory under the guidance of Giovanni Cassini. Rømer's work included precisely timing the orbit of Jupiter's moon, Io. In the late seventeenth century, sailors used Io's orbit to set their clocks at sea. These clock corrections allowed for more accurate navigation.

Over the course of several years, Rømer noticed that Io's orbit appeared to speed up and slow down slightly, depending on where Jupiter appeared in the sky.

When Jupiter is at opposition—highest in the sky at midnight—it is closest to Earth. When Jupiter is near conjunction—close to the sun in our sky—it is farthest from Earth.

Rømer found that Io appeared a few minutes "ahead of schedule" when Jupiter was at opposition. When Jupiter was near conjunction, Io appeared a few minutes "behind schedule." Rømer came to believe this was caused by the distance light had to travel. When Io was closer, the light from it arrived at Earth sooner. When Io was more distant, the light arrived later.

Fellow Dutch scientist Christiaan Huygens was an early supporter of Rømer's idea. Using Rømer's timings of Io, and Cassini's measurement of the Astronomical Unit (see How Far Away Is the Sun? page 88), Huygens calculated the speed of light to be about 133,000 miles per second—a little less than our modern measurement of 186,282 miles per second.

Orbits of Jupiter and Earth

WHEN DID THE UNIVERSE BEGIN?

Have you ever noticed that when an emergency vehicle is approaching, its siren sounds higher pitched, but when it's moving away, it sounds lower? This is called the Doppler effect, named for German scientist Christian Doppler who first described it in 1842.

We experience the Doppler effect whenever a source of waves, like sound waves, is moving toward or away from us. When the source is approaching, its waves get bunched together and we observe them at a higher frequency. When the source is moving away, waves get spread out and we observe them at lower frequency.

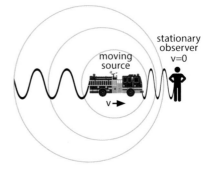

Try this for yourself. If you listen to a car driving by on a highway, you will hear its engine sound higher pitched as it approaches and lower pitched as it speeds away. It sounds a bit like "EEEEEEEYAHHHHH." The effect is even more pronounced with the sirens on emergency vehicles.

Light is also a wave, and red light has a lower frequency than blue light. When a source of light moves away from us, we see it at a lower frequency—it looks redder. Scientists say it appears "red shifted." When a source of light moves toward us, you guessed it, it appears "blue shifted." The faster the source of light is moving, the more it will appear red or blue shifted.

In the early 1900s, astronomer Vesto Slipher studied the spectra (the rainbow of colors visible when light passes through a prism) of galaxies and found that almost every galaxy in the sky appeared red shifted. Most galaxies were moving away from us.

In the 1920s, Edwin Hubble expanded on Slipher's work and noticed something else. The farther away a galaxy was, the greater its red shift. Distant galaxies were moving away faster than nearby galaxies. In 1929, Hubble published his explanation of these observations: the entire universe was expanding.

Soon after, a young physicist named Georges Lemaître took Hubble's insight one step further. He imagined the expanding universe like a movie, then ran the movie backwards. All the galaxies would be rushing toward one another. Eventually, they would all be packed together into a single point—the beginning of the universe. Lemaître's theory became poetically known as the "Big Bang."

Using careful measurements of the red shift of distant galaxies, astronomers calculate that this "Big Bang" took place about 13.7 billion years ago.

ARE WE ALONE IN THE UNIVERSE?

In December 1990, the *Galileo* spacecraft flew past Earth on its way to Jupiter. As it did, it ran a test to find out if a space probe could detect life on a planet.

Earth is the only planet where scientists have detected life. So far.

It worked. *Galileo* detected clear signs of life on Earth.

In addition to vast areas of liquid water, the probe measured a large amount of oxygen in the atmosphere and saw specific colors of sunlight being absorbed across most of the land. *Galileo* was seeing not only oceans, but also the signs of plants soaking up sunlight and releasing oxygen. No known non-living process could explain *Galileo's* observations.

For most of human history, Earth was the only world people knew. After the invention of the telescope in 1609, scientists came to understand that the planets in our sky are also worlds. This raised the question— was there life on these other worlds? The question has captured the imagination of both scientists and non-scientists ever since.

Scientists search for life by looking for two things: the conditions needed to support life and signs of life that cannot be explained by non-living processes.

One basic requirement for life as we know it is liquid water. In the early seventeenth century, many astronomers thought that the mosaic of light and dark patches on the moon were continents and oceans. They named the dark patches *maria*, which is Latin for "seas." As telescopes improved, it became clear that the *maria* were simply darker patches of ground, not oceans of water. In 1753, Roger Boscovich showed that the moon did not have an atmosphere (see The Surface of the Moon page 34). After this, few people believed the moon could support life and the search turned to Mars.

In 1877, the Italian astronomer Giovanni Schiaparelli reported seeing lines on the surface of Mars. He called these lines *canali* in Italian, meaning "channels." Many English speakers through he meant "canals" and went looking for artificial waterways on Mars. In 1893, the eccentric American businessman and amateur astronomer Percival Lowell constructed an observatory in Arizona to study Mars. Even with the best telescopes of the day, it was difficult to see features on Mars. Even so, Lowell became convinced that the "canals" were real and that they must have been built by an alien civilization. Despite a lack of solid evidence, he wrote several books on the subject that captured public imagination and fueled a search for life on Mars that continues today. In the early 1960s, photos from the *Mariner* space probes in orbit around Mars showed that Schiaparelli's *canali* were an optical illusion. In the 1970s, the *Viking* landers sampled Martian soil and found no evidence of the chemistry of life. Most scientists today believe that Mars does not support life—but many still wonder if it did in the ancient past.

Astronomers still search for water as a basic requirement for life. They also look for the chemicals needed for life as we know it. Scientists continue to send probes to Mars, and to moons of Jupiter and Saturn, to look for signs of life—including signs of ancient life that may have died out long ago.

Astronomers also search for worlds orbiting other stars—exoplanets—that might support life. These worlds are too far away for spacecraft to visit, but astronomers can estimate how hot they are based on how close they are to their star. If a planet is too hot, any water would boil away. Too cold, and water would freeze. Astronomers also use stellar spectroscopy (the

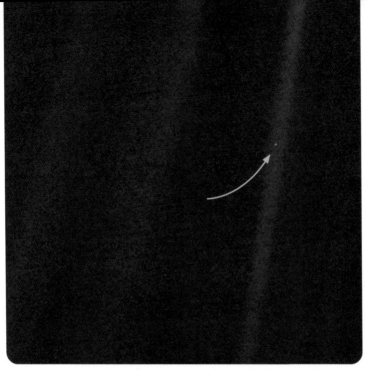

The Earth as seen from billions of miles away by the
Voyager 1 spacecraft; we are the tiny bluish dot.

careful study of starlight, see What Are Stars Made Of? page 97) to look for chemicals on distant worlds—just like *Galileo* did when it flew past Earth.

The more they search, the more astronomers find evidence that planets, water, and the chemicals needed for life are common in the universe. So common that it seems likely that life exists elsewhere. But we have not found it. No study of other worlds has yet found what *Galileo* saw as it flew past Earth—liquid water and signs of life that cannot be explained by other processes.

Ursa Minor

Ursa Major

Cancer

Boötes

Leo

Virgo

Tours of the Night Sky

SPRING TOUR

The spring sky is dominated by the Big Dipper, one of the best-known star patterns in the sky. These bright, familiar stars will guide us across the spring sky.

- The stars of the Big Dipper are part of the constellation Ursa Major, the Great Bear.

- The front edge of the "ladle" or "dipper" points to Polaris, the North Star, in Ursa Minor, the Little Bear.

- The arcing handle of the Big Dipper guides us to the bright-orange star Arcturus (arc-TOUR-russ) in Boötes (bo-OH-teez), and pearly white Spica in Virgo.

- The back edge of the ladle points toward the star Regulus in Leo.

- From Leo, we can spot the faint stars of the constellation Cancer.

THE BIG DIPPER

Let's begin by taking a closer look at one of the stars in the Big Dipper. There is more here than meets the eye—and that's often true for other objects in the night sky.

The bright star in the middle of the handle is called Mizar. Next to Mizar is a slightly dimmer star named Alcor. Many ancient cultures used these stars as a vision test. Next time you see the Big Dipper, see if you can spot dimmer Alcor next to bright Mizar.

Mizar and Alcor don't just appear close together in the sky. Many scientists believe they are bound together by gravity. But there is even more here than we can see with our eyes alone. In the early 1600s, Italian scholar Benedetto Castelli used the newly invented telescope to discover another, closer companion to Mizar. If you have a telescope, try spotting Mizar B, next to brighter Mizar A.

A little over 100 years ago, astronomers used the new science of stellar spectroscopy (the careful study of color in starlight) to show that Mizar A and Mizar B are each binary stars themselves. And in 2009, scientists searching for exoplanets discovered another star orbiting close to Alcor. It turns out that Mizar and Alcor are a six-star system!

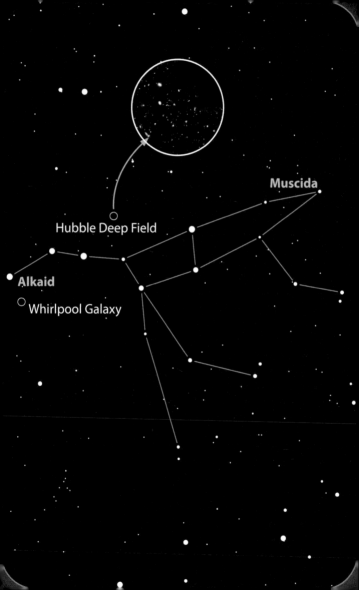

Muscida

Hubble Deep Field

Alkaid

Whirlpool Galaxy

URSA MAJOR: THE GREAT BEAR

The Big Dipper is part of the constellation Ursa Major, the Great Bear. Can you make out the shape of the bear in the sky? It has a pointed snout, long legs and, oddly, a long tail. (In real life, bears have short tails.)

The spring sky gives us a window into the distant universe. In 1995, the Hubble Space Telescope took a long-exposure photograph of a tiny area of "empty" space in Ursa Major. The photograph revealed thousands of distant galaxies as they appeared billions of years ago. The image helped astronomers understand how galaxies formed in the early universe.

Closer to home is M51, the Whirlpool Galaxy, which is visible in a small telescope. With clear skies and excellent eyesight, you may be able to spot it in a pair of binoculars. To find M51, "hop" east then south from Alkaid, the star marking the tip of the bear's tail.

If you want to see the home of an exoplanet closer to the Earth, take a look at Muscida, the star that marks the tip of the bear's nose. In 2012, a team of scientists in Japan discovered a large planet orbiting around Muscida.

M51, the Whirlpool Galaxy

THE WHIRLPOOL GALAXY

M51, also known as the Whirlpool Galaxy, is a spiral galaxy in the constellation Canes Venatici, the Hunting Dogs. The galaxy was first recorded by Charles Messier in 1773. Eight years later, Pierre Méchain reported a second, smaller galaxy next to M51. Scientists now know that the galaxies are actually brushing past one another. How do they know? As gravity from the smaller galaxy pulls on M51, it causes new stars to form in clouds of gas and dust. The gas and dust appear red in this image. Hot, young stars appear blue.

M51 is also a popular target for amateur astronomers. Under dark skies, M51 may be visible in binoculars as a small smudge of light. A small telescope reveals both galaxies in some detail—but it is too dim for us to see any color with our own eyes.

In September 2021, a team of scientists led by Dr. Rosanne Di Stefano announced evidence of an exoplanet in the Whirlpool Galaxy (M51). If confirmed, this will be the first planet discovered in another galaxy.

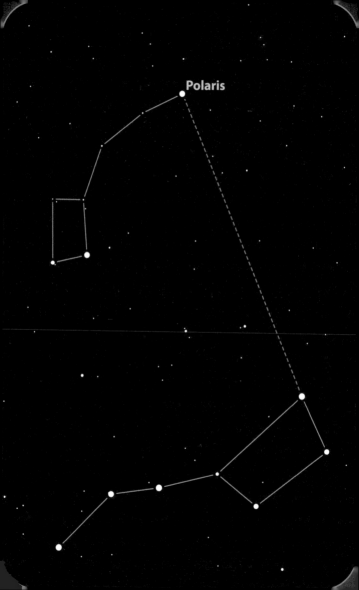

THE NORTH STAR AND THE LITTLE DIPPER

Polaris, also called the North Star, is the one star that never appears to move in our sky. As the Earth rotates, all of the other stars in the sky seem to circle around Polaris. Polaris lies almost directly above the Earth's north pole, and it has been used by travelers for centuries to find true north.

To find Polaris, follow the "pointer stars" on the front edge of the Big Dipper to the next bright star.

Polaris is in the constellation Ursa Minor, the Little Bear. The pattern of stars is also called the Little Dipper. Polaris marks the tip of the handle of the Little Dipper. Most of the other stars in the Little Dipper are not as bright as Polaris. In fact, looking at the Little Dipper is a good way to figure out how dark your sky is. If you can only see one or two stars in the bowl, the sky is fairly bright. You may have a hard time seeing constellations. If you can easily see all four stars in the bowl, the sky is quite dark. You should be able to see every star shown on these charts, as well as brighter star clusters, nebulae, and galaxies.

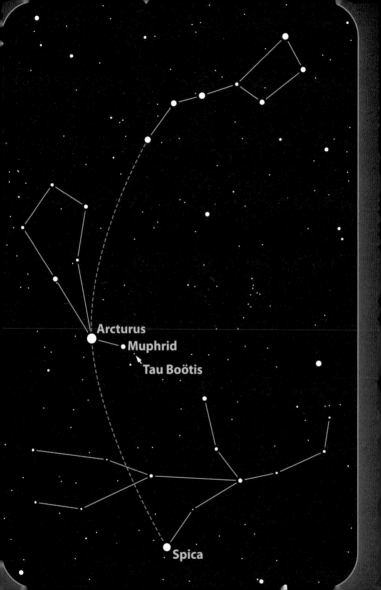

Arcturus

Muphrid

Tau Boötis

Spica

ARC TO ARCTURUS AND SPEED ON TO SPICA

Arcturus is the brightest star in the northern half of the sky. It marks the base of the constellation Boötes (bo-OH-teez). The stars of Boötes look like a lop-sided kite. Arcturus is easy to spot. Follow the arc of the Dipper's handle across the sky to Arcturus.

Close to Arcturus is a star called Muphrid. Arcturus and Muphrid are the same distance from the Earth and close together in space. We don't know of any planets orbiting Muphrid. If one exists, Arcturus would shine as brightly in its sky as the crescent moon does in ours. Imagine a star so bright it casts shadows at night!

Close to Muphrid in the sky is a dim star called Tau Boötis. Circling around that star is one of the first exoplanets ever discovered. Researchers at the San Francisco Planet Search Project measured tiny wobbles in the position of the star. The wobbles are caused by the pull of a massive planet circling the star.

Spica is the only bright star in the constellation Virgo. If you continue the curve from the Dipper through Arcturus, it will point you to Spica. Speed on to Spica. Virgo is the largest constellation in the zodiac. The sun spends more time in Virgo than in any other constellation.

Sickle

Algieba

40 Leonis

Regulus

LEO

The stars on the back edge of the Big Dipper point toward the zodiac constellation Leo. Leo's brightest star, Regulus, lies just off the ecliptic and is frequently seen near the moon or one of the planets.

In fact, every nine years the moon will pass directly in front of Regulus each month for more than a year. Astronomers use these events, called occultations, to measure the position of the moon with great precision. The next series will begin in July of 2025. It can be a challenge to spot these occultations. Not every occulation is visible from every spot on earth, each lasts just a few moments, and some take place during the daytime.

Regulus marks the base of a pattern of stars called the Sickle, which looks like a backward question mark. In the middle of the Sickle is a star called Algieba. If you look closely, you may be able to spot the star 40 Leonis close to Algieba. These two stars form an optical double. They appear close together in the sky, but Algieba is more than twice as far away.

A telescope reveals that Algieba itself is a double star. And it's not just an optical double, it's a true binary star system. The brighter of the two stars may also have at least one exoplanet. In 2009, astronomers measured tiny wobbles in the position of Algieba A that could be caused by the gravitational tug of a planet about twice the size of Jupiter orbiting the star.

Sickle

Praesepe

CANCER AND THE BEEHIVE CLUSTER (THE PRAESEPE)

Just west of the Sickle of Leo are the faint stars of the constellation Cancer. Though dim, Cancer is well known as one of the constellations of the zodiac. The sun is in Cancer from July 19 to August 7 each year, and the moon and planets all pass through this area of the sky.

Cancer is also home to a beautiful cluster of stars called the Praesepe, or M44. Under dark skies, the Praesepe is visible to the naked eye as a faint, fuzzy patch of light. Binoculars reveal a dense group of stars that seem to swarm like bees. The Praesepe was one of the first things that Galileo observed with the newly invented telescope in 1609. His discovery that there were many more stars than the eye alone could see helped pave the way for the scientific revolution of the seventeenth century.

Today, astronomers know that the Praesepe is about 600 light-years away from Earth and that at least two of the stars in the cluster have planets orbiting them.

Cygnus

Lyra

Hercules

Aquila

Capricornus

Sagittarius

Libra

Scorpius

SUMMER TOUR

On summer evenings, a trio of bright stars frames the band of the Milky Way and provides a prominent landmark for navigating the summer sky.

- The Summer Triangle is made up of the brightest stars from three different constellations: Cygnus, Lyra, and Aquila.

- The long line of Cygnus points along the Milky Way toward the constellations Sagittarius and Scorpius.

- The top edge of the triangle points west to Hercules.

- The western edge of the triangle points south to the dim zodiac constellation Capricornus.

Summer is also when we have some of our strongest meteor activity—adding the unpredictable treat of a "shooting star" to a summer evening spent watching the night sky.

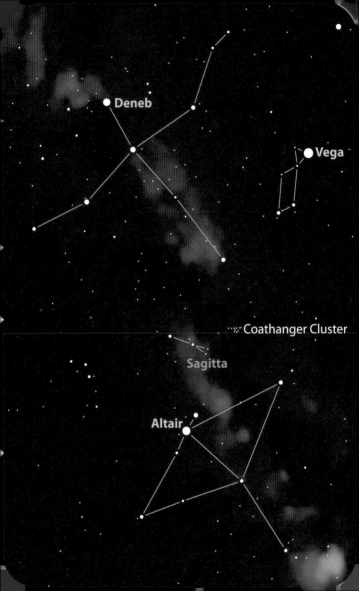

THE SUMMER TRIANGLE

The Summer Triangle is a trio of bright stars that frame the Milky Way: Deneb in Cygnus, Vega in Lyra, and Altair in Aquila. These stars mark some of the most prominent constellations in the summer sky, and serve as a guide to the rest.

The Milky Way is a wonderful area to scan with binoculars, and the Summer Triangle is a great place to start.

Near the middle of the Summer Triangle is one of the smallest constellations in the sky, Sagitta, the arrow. Though tiny and not very bright, its distinct, compact shape makes it easy to pick out. It is so small, you can see all its bright stars at once through wide-field binoculars.

Just west of Sagitta is another delightful star pattern, CR 399, the Coathanger cluster. This open star cluster is visible to the naked eye as a faint, fuzzy spot in the Milky Way. Binoculars reveal a tiny star cluster that looks like a miniature wooden coat hanger.

CYGNUS

Deneb marks the "tail" of the constellation Cygnus, the swan. Although Deneb appears to us as the dimmest star in the Summer Triangle, it is actually one of the most luminous stars in the entire galaxy. It appears dimmer than Vega and Altair because it is believed to be more than 2,600 light-years from Earth. Altair, by contrast, is only 17 light-years away. If Deneb were the same distance as Altair, it would appear as bright as a crescent moon and be visible during the day.

The head of the swan is marked by Alberio, one of the most beautiful double stars in the sky and a favorite of amateur astronomers. Some sharp-eyed observers can split the two stars with binoculars.

Midway along the swan's neck is a remarkable variable star called Chi Cygni. Over a period of about a year, Chi Cygni can brighten and dim by 10,000 times. At its brightest, it can be seen with the naked eye. At its dimmest, it is invisible in small telescopes.

Cygnus is also home to 61 Cygni—the first star whose distance was measured by parallax. Though barely visible to the naked eye, this star played a big role in the history of astronomy. Friedrich Bessel's announcement in 1838 that 61 Cygni was more than ten light-years away showed that stars were distant suns. And that meant our sun was simply one of countless suns in an unimaginably large universe.

Double-Double

Vega

Sheliak

Ring Nebula

LYRA

The constellation Lyra is marked by the brilliant blue-white star Vega—one of the brightest stars in the sky. Lyra is one of the smaller constellations and looks like a triangle balanced on a parallelogram, like a pair of Tangram tiles.

Next to Vega at the top of the triangle is the star Epsilon Lyrae, better known as the Double-Double. Binoculars, or exceptional eyesight, reveal two nearly identical looking stars close together. A good telescope makes it clear that each of these is itself a double star. These stars are not a chance line-of-sight pairing, but a true multi-star system.

Along the bottom of the parallelogram is the star Sheliak. Though it too looks like a single star, even through a telescope, Sheliak is an eclipsing binary. As the two stars orbit one another, each blocks some of the other's light, which causes the system to dim and then brighten again twice during each 13-day orbit. By carefully comparing Sheliak to nearby stars, you may be able to detect these eclipses yourself.

Near Sheliak is a faint object called M57, the Ring Nebula. Too dim to see with the naked eye, M57 is a planetary nebula—a glowing shell of gas cast off by a dying star. In a small telescope, M57 looks like a tiny circle. Large telescopes reveal beautiful detail and may even show the faint, fading star at the center.

Antares

M4

M7

SCORPIUS AND LIBRA

The neck of the swan points halfway across the sky toward the bright orange star Antares in the zodiac constellation Scorpius, the scorpion. Antares lies close to the ecliptic and is often seen near the moon or planets. Its bright-orange color is similar to that of Mars. In fact, the name Antares means "like Mars" in Greek.

Just to the west of Antares is the globular cluster M4. Under clear, dark skies, M4 may be visible to the naked eye as a faint, fuzzy star. A good telescope reveals some of the cluster's more than 100,000 individual stars. In addition to the stars we can see through a telescope, M4 contains tens of thousands of white dwarfs—fading remnants of ancient stars that used up their nuclear fuel long ago. These white dwarfs are believed to be some of the oldest stars in the universe—up to 13 billion years old.

To the west of Scorpius is a group of fainter stars that make up the zodiac constellation Libra. In ancient times, these stars were considered part of Scorpius, marking the "claws" of the scorpion.

Opposite Libra, near the tip of the scorpion's tail, is the rich star cluster M7, sometimes known as the Ptolemy Star cluster. It is easily visible to the naked eye under dark skies and spectacular in a small telescope.

Keystone

M13

HERCULES

A line across the top of the Summer Triangle points to the constellation Hercules. The easiest way to find Hercules is to look for the pattern of stars called the Keystone, which will look a little smaller than your fist held at arm's length.

About a third of the way down the right edge of the Keystone is M13, one of the brightest globular clusters in the sky. It is a good challenge to spot with the naked eye, looking like a dim "star" that appears fuzzy rather than sharp. It is one of the finest objects in the sky to view through a small telescope. M13 is 22,200 light-years from Earth. It contains about 300,000 stars clustered in a sphere some 84 light-years across.

Milky Way

Eagle Nebula

Sagittarius Star Cloud

SAGITTARIUS

Just east of the tail of the scorpion are the stars of the zodiac constellation Sagittarius, the archer. Although these stars look a bit like a bow being drawn back, they look even more like a teapot to most stargazers.

Rising like steam from the spout of the teapot are the rich star fields of the Milky Way. When we look in this direction, we are looking toward the center of our own galaxy. This area of space is filled with interstellar dust and gas, limiting how far we can see. But there is one "window" through all this dust that offers an unobstructed view for 16,000 light-years. M24, also known as the Sagittarius Star Cloud, is one of the densest patches of stars in our sky. It is visible to the naked eye as a dim cloud-like region a little above the top of the teapot. Seen through binoculars, about 1,000 stars are visible in a single field of view.

Above M24 in the neighboring constellation Serpens is M16, the Eagle Nebula. It can be seen in binoculars as a faint, fuzzy spot. A small telescope shows a loose open cluster of stars. Larger telescopes show a large area of gas and dust illuminated by hot, young stars.

The famous Hubble image of the Pillars of Creation

THE PILLARS OF CREATION

M16, the Eagle Nebula, is a favorite target for astro-photographers—people who take photographs of the night sky. Long-exposure photos can reveal details, especially colors, that our eyes cannot detect in real time. Photos of M16 show colorful clouds of gas illuminated by brilliant blue stars. And the most famous photograph ever taken of M16 shows even more.

In 1995, the Hubble Space Telescope imaged a small area near the center of M16. A similar image was taken 20 years later with an upgraded camera. The Hubble images showed towering fingers of gas and dust 4–5 light-years in length lit up by a group of bright stars just outside the picture. These fingers contain dense globules of gas where new stars are forming, giving them the nickname the Pillars of Creation. Besides being among the most stunning astrophotos ever taken, the Hubble images have helped astronomers learn more about the process of star formation.

FALL TOUR

On fall evenings, the Great Square of Pegasus serves as our guide to the sky. Though not exceptionally bright, the Great Square frames a relatively empty region, making it one of the most prominent features in the fall sky—and an excellent guide for our tour.

- The right-hand edge points up to Cepheus.
- The left-hand edge points up to Cassiopeia.
- The northeast corner of the Square marks the beginning of Andromeda.
- The bright arc of stars in Andromeda points to Perseus.
- The dim stars of Pisces wrap around the south and east sides of the Great Square.
- Aries lies to the east of the Great Square, beyond Pisces.
- A diagonal line through the Square points southwest to Aquarius.

THE GREAT SQUARE

The Great Square outlines the body of the constellation Pegasus, the mythical horse. The horse appears upside down, facing to the right. One chain of stars marks its head and neck. Dimmer stars mark the front legs.

WORLDS ORBITING A DISTANT SUN

About halfway down the western (right hand) side of the Great Square—near the top of the horse's sternum—is a faint star called, 51 Pegasi, also known as Helvetios. Though it is quite an average star, and barely visible to the naked eye, 51 Pegasi made headlines in 1995 and changed the course of modern astronomy.

That year, a team of Swiss scientists discovered an exoplanet orbiting the star. How do they know? The planet was discovered by observing tiny wobbles in the star's position caused by the gravitational pull of the planet. It was the first time an exoplanet had been found around a star similar to our sun, and it set off a wave of exoplanet surveys that continue to this day.

In 2019, the team was awarded the Nobel Prize in Physics for their discovery.

You will need clear, dark skies to see 51 Pegasi with your naked eye. Under typical suburban skies, you can spot it with a pair of binoculars.

Navi

Mu Cephei

Zeta Cephei

Delta Cephei

Epsilon Cephei

CASSIOPEIA AND CEPHEUS

Sitting above the Great Square are the constellations Cassiopeia and Cepheus. Bright Cassiopeia looks like a wide "W." Dim Cepheus looks a bit like a young child's drawing of a house.

The five stars that form the "W" of Cassiopeia are about as bright as the stars of the Big Dipper. But the star at the center of the "W" doesn't have a traditional name. In the 1960s, astronaut Virgil Ivan "Gus" Grissom nicknamed this star Navi because it was used for navigation. It's also his own middle name spelled backwards. The name caught on and is now officially recognized.

Delta Cephei is the star that Cepheid variables are named for. Astronomers use these stars to measure vast cosmic distances (see How Far Away Are Other Galaxies? page 92). It's tricky, but possible, to track Delta Cephei's changing brightness by comparing it to nearby stars. Over a period of a little more than five days, Delta Cephei grows as bright as nearby Zeta Cephei and fades as dim as neighboring Epsilon.

Mu Cephei is faintly visible to the naked eye under dark skies. But in binoculars or a small telescope, the star shines a brilliant deep red. Astronomers believe Mu Cephei is a supergiant star nearing the end of its life.

ANDROMEDA

The star Alpheratz marks the northeast (upper-left) corner of the Great Square. It also marks the tip of the narrow, curving "A" shape of the constellation Andromeda. Historically, the star was sometimes considered part of both constellations. Today, it is officially part of Andromeda.

Andromeda is home to M31, the Andromeda Galaxy, the most distant object in the universe easily visible to the naked eye. A spiral galaxy similar to our own Milky Way, M31 is 2.5 million light-years from Earth. When we look at M31, we are seeing light emitted from its stars 2.5 million years ago.

To find M31, first find Mirach along the lower line of stars forming the A of Andromeda. Look above Mirach for the next visible star, Mu Andromedae, and continue that same distance again. M31 appears as a faint, fuzzy oval.

The Andromeda Galaxy through a large telescope

THE ANDROMEDA GALAXY

M31 has been known to stargazers since before recorded history. But it was just 100 years ago that it was first recognized as a galaxy, like our own Milky Way.

From ancient times until the beginning of the twentieth century, this object was known in western science as the Andromeda nebula. It was believed to be a cloud of gas, similar to other fuzzy patches in the sky.

In 1924, Edwin Hubble used Henrietta Swan Leavitt's method of measuring distance using Cepheid variable stars to show that M31 was more than a million light-years from Earth (see How Far Away Are Other Galaxies? page 92). This discovery showed that M31 was an entire galaxy and that the universe was much bigger than previously imagined.

M31 is easy to see under clear, dark skies. Binoculars will show some of the galaxy's spiral structure and the bright bulge at its center. A telescope will reveal even more detail.

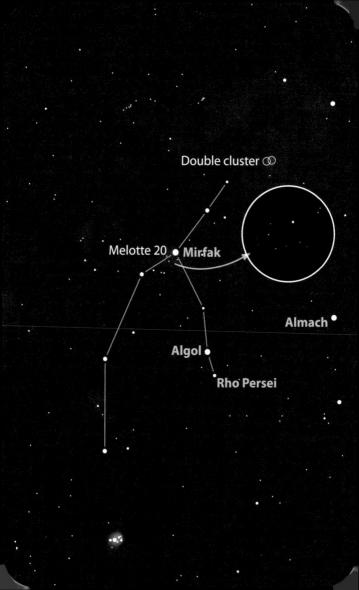

PERSEUS

The curving shape of Andromeda points toward the bright star Mirfak in the constellation Perseus.

Mirfak is part of a cluster of stars known as Melotte 20. Under clear, dark skies, you can see a few stars in this cluster. Binoculars will reveal dozens, and a medium-sized telescope can show hundreds. Most of the stars in the cluster are hotter than our sun and shine bright blue.

Located near Cassiopeia are two faint, fuzzy patches of light, just visible to the naked eye. Together they are known as the Double cluster. Binoculars reveal a pair of rich star clusters, each about the size of the full moon.

Perseus is also home to one of the most famous variable stars in the sky—the transiting binary star Algol. A transiting binary is a pair of stars that regularly eclipse one another, blocking some of their light. Eclipses of Algol happen about once every three days and last for about ten hours. It is possible to track these eclipses by comparing the brightness of Algol to other, nearby stars. Algol is usually a little brighter than Almach in the constellation Androm-eda. During an eclipse, Algol grows a bit dimmer than neighboring Rho Persei. Astronomers use similar dips in brightness to detect exoplanets around distant stars (see Exoplanets page 65).

Hamal

First Point of Aries

AQUARIUS, PISCES, ARIES

Three constellations of the zodiac are visible in the fall sky. These are the constellations where we see the moon and planets.

Pisces is a large, dim constellation that wraps around the south and east sides of the Great Square. The sun is in the constellation Pisces on the first day of spring. The exact location of the sun when spring begins is, somewhat confusingly, called The First Point of Aires. This is an old name that dates back thousands of years to a time when the sun appeared in Aries on the first day of spring.

Aries is the easiest fall zodiac constellation to spot. It is marked by two relatively bright stars a bit more than a hand-span to the east (left) of the Great Square. Astronomers have detected exoplanets orbiting around Hamal, the brightest star in Aries.

Aquarius is another large, dim constellation located south and west of the Great Square. A diagonal line through the square runs along the top of this dim, sprawling constellation.

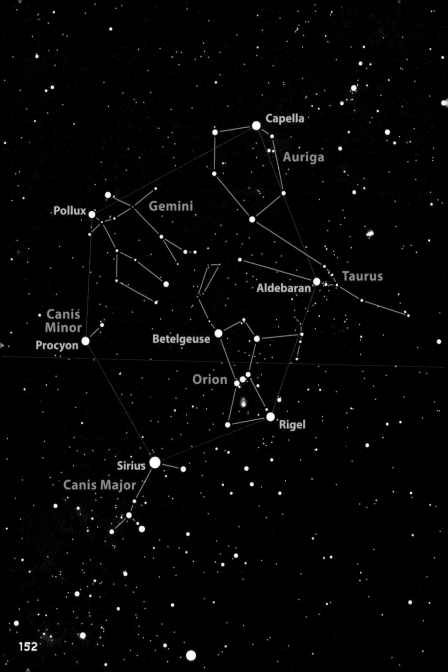

WINTER TOUR

Seven of the fourteen brightest stars visible from most of the United States are highest in the sky on winter evenings. These bright stars from a huge pattern in the sky known as the Great Hexagon.

- Bright-orange Betelgeuse marks the center of the Great Hexagon.
- The three stars of Orion's Belt point left to Sirius, the brightest star in the sky.
- Circling clockwise, the corners of the Great Hexagon are marked by:
    - Sirius in Canis Major
    - Procyon in Canis Minor
    - Pollux in Gemini
    - Capella in Auriga
    - Aldebaran in Taurus
    - Rigel in Orion

Betelgeuse

Orion Nebula (M42)

Rigel

ORION

Orion contains more bright stars than any other constellation and has a compact, easily recognizable shape. Its most prominent stars are brilliant blue Rigel, fiery red Betelgeuse, and the trio of stars that form "Orion's Belt."

Rigel is not only one of the brightest stars in the sky, it is also one of the most luminous stars known. Parallax measurements from the *Gaia* space telescope put Rigel 863 light-years from Earth. At that distance, Rigel must be more than 20 times the mass of our sun and 120,000 times as luminous.

Betelgeuse is a variable star with a period of about four weeks. You can track these variations yourself by comparing it to other stars in the Great Hexagon. At its usual maximum, Betelgeuse shines as bright as Procyon in the constellation Canis Minor. At its usual minimum, it appears just a little dimmer than Pollux in Gemini. Occasionally, Betelgeuse varies even more, shining brighter than Rigel or growing as dim as the stars of Orion's Belt.

How do you pronounce Betelgeuse? Some astronomers say "beetle-juice" while other insist that it should be "bet-el-jooze." Which do you like more?

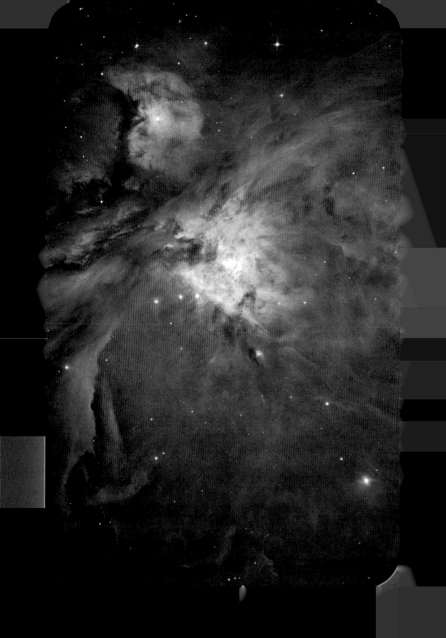

THE ORION NEBULA

M42, also known as the Orion Nebula, is one of the brightest nebulae in the sky. It is visible to the naked eye, even in areas with modest light pollution. The nebula is a stellar nursery, roughly 1,340 light-years from Earth. Astronomers study the nebula to learn how new stars form.

The Orion Nebula was the first deep sky object ever photographed and has been a popular target for amateur and professional astrophotographers ever since. Henry Draper took the first photo of M42 in 1880 from his home observatory in Greenburgh, New York. In the decades the followed, astronomers used photography and spectroscopy to study M42 in great detail.

Since 1993, the nebula has been a frequent target for the Hubble Space Telescope. Astronomers have used Hubble's images to create a three-dimensional model of the nebula, observe more than 600 new stars in various stages of forming, and even see how planets begin to form around young stars.

You don't need a space telescope or your own observatory to photograph the Orion Nebula. You can get a pretty good picture through nearly any telescope using a smartphone. Just line your camera lens up with the telescope eyepiece and snap away.

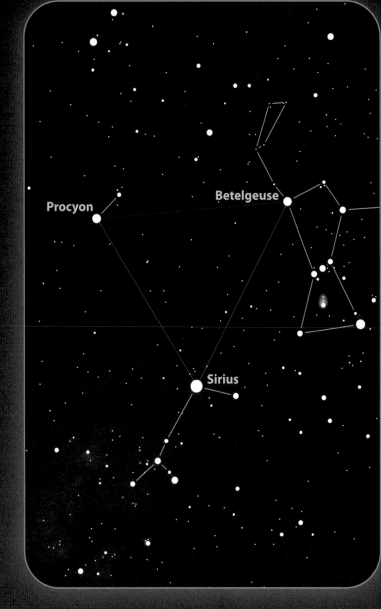

THE WINTER TRIANGLE

The stars Sirius, Procyon, and Betelgeuse are known together as the Winter Triangle.

Sirius, in the constellation Canis Major, is the brightest star in our sky. It is more than twice as bright as any other star, and more than four times as bright as other stars in the Great Hexagon. The only objects that appear brighter in the sky are part of our own solar system. Unlike Rigel or Betelgeuse, Sirius is not a particularly large or luminous star. It appears so bright because it is extremely close—just 8.8 light-years from Earth. Sirius means "Searing" in Greek and this brilliant star's morning rising was thought to bring on the "dog days" of summer. From this, Sirius got the nickname "the dog star."

Procyon is the eighth-brightest star in the sky and marks the northeast corner of the Winter Triangle. Like Sirius it is also a close neighbor, lying 11.4 light-years away. The star's name means "before the dog" in Greek. Procyon rises above the horizon shortly before Sirius—coming into view just before the "dog star."

Between the bright stars of the Winter Triangle is the dim constellation Monoceros, the Unicorn. Though Monoceros has no bright stars, the Milky Way passes through the center of this constellation. It is full of faint star clusters and nebulae and is a wonderful area to scan with binoculars.

Castor

Pollux

GEMINI

Gemini, which means "twins" in Greek, is easy to spot because of its two bright stars, Pollux and Castor. A line traced from Rigel through Betelgeuse points toward these bright twins.

Pollux is the brighter of the two stars, and the 17th-brightest star in the sky. Using parallax measurements from the *Gaia* space telescope, astronomers calculate that Pollux is 34 light-years from Earth, making it a fairly close neighbor. In 1993, astronomers observed tiny wobbles in the position of Pollux that they suspected were caused by an exoplanet. In 2006, more-precise measurements confirmed the existence of the exoplanet, which was named Thestias.

To the naked eye, Castor looks like a single star. A telescope reveals that it is a close optical double. By carefully measuring their movements over many years, astronomers have concluded that these two stars are in orbit around one another, and that a third, fainter star seen nearby is also part of the system. Spectroscopic studies have revealed that each of these three stars are actually close binaries. Castor is a six-star system!

AURIGA

The top of the Great Hexagon is marked by Capella in the constellation Auriga. Auriga itself is shaped a bit like a hexagon, making it pretty easy to identify. It encircles a stretch of the Milky Way, making it a rich area to observe through binoculars.

Capella is the brightest star in Auriga and the northernmost of all the first-magnitude stars. It is so far north that it is visible for at least part of every night of the year from most of the United States.

Located just a little southwest of Capella is a star called Almaaz, also known as Epsilon Aurigae. Though it does not appear exceptionally bright, it is believed to be one of the most luminous stars in our region of the galaxy. Measurements from the *Gaia* space telescope suggest that Almaaz is roughly 3,300 light-years from Earth. To appear as bright as it does at this distance, Almaaz must be about 38,000 times as luminous as our sun.

Almaaz is also an unusual eclipsing variable. Once every 27 years, the star dims for a period of two years as something passes in front of it, blocking part of its light from our view. From 2009 to 2011, professional and amateur astronomers all over the world made detailed observations of the most recent eclipse. Despite this intensive study, the nature of the system remains a mystery.

Elnath

Crab Nebula

Pleiades

Aldebaran

Hyades

A line traced through Orion's Belt points west toward Taurus and two of the most prominent star clusters in the sky, the Hyades and the Pleiades. These two clusters are so large that they are best viewed with binoculars. Most telescopes offer too small a view.

The Hyades, also known as Melotte 25, is a large, loose star cluster located just west of Aldebaran. The brightest stars in the cluster from a triangle that marks the head of the bull, Taurus. Bright-red Aldebaran marks the bull's-eye. The cluster is easy to see with the naked eye under clear, dark skies and great to view in binoculars.

The Pleiades, cataloged as M45, is the most famous star cluster in the sky. It is easy to spot with the naked eye. A person with good eyesight can see six or more stars clustered in a fuzzy patch about four times the diameter of the full moon.

Near the tip of the bull's lower horn is M1, the Crab Nebula. M1 is a supernova remnant—the expanding shell of gas and debris blasted out into space by an exploding star. It is too faint to see with the naked eye, but it is visible in binoculars as a small, faint blotch of light. A good telescope will show some texture and the nebula's egg-like shape.

The Pleiades through the Hubble space telescope

THE PLEIADES

M45 is the most famous star cluster in the sky and was recognized by ancient cultures across the world. This prominent, compact grouping of stars features in the folklore of the Celtic, Cherokee, Chinese, Japanese, Māori, Mayan, and Persian peoples, to name just a few. In ancient Greece, the stars were known as the Pleiades.

Most people can make out six stars in the cluster with their naked eyes, though some sharp-eyed observers can spot as many as 14. The first person to observe the Pleiades through a telescope was the Italian astronomer Galileo Galilei. In 1610, he published a sketch of the cluster showing 35 stars, far more than anyone could see with their eyes alone. A pair of binoculars will reveal even more stars than Galileo saw. Binoculars may even reveal a hint of nebulosity—the soft glow around the bright stars caused by their light reflecting off interstellar dust.

Astronomers have counted over 1,000 stars that are part of the cluster. Most of the light of the cluster comes from bright, blue-white stars. But observations with high-powered telescopes, including the Hubble space telescope, suggest that most of the cluster's mass comes from faint, red stars.

Glossary

Asteroid: A rocky body, smaller than a planet, in a direct orbit around the sun.

Astronomer: A professional or amateur who studies astronomy.

Astronomy: The scientific study of things beyond the Earth, like stars, planets, moons, comets, and galaxies.

Binary Star: Two stars that are gravitationally bound to each other.

Binoculars: A handheld instrument made of two small telescopes joined together that offers modest magnification, a large field of view, and an upright image.

Cepheid Variables: A type of variable star that can be used as a standard candle to measure distance in astronomy.

Comet: Small objects made of ice and dust in orbit around the sun. Most comets orbit beyond Neptune. Occasionally, a comet will enter the inner solar system and be visible from Earth.

Constellation: A visual grouping of stars that defines a specific area of our sky. Every point in the sky belongs to one, and only one, constellation.

Deep Sky Object: An observable object other than individual stars that exist beyond our solar system. Examples include nebulae, star clusters, and galaxies.

Double Star: Two stars that appear close together in the sky. Double stars can be either true multi-star systems or chance line-of-sight pairings known as optical doubles.

Dwarf Planet: An object in orbit around a star that has enough gravity to compress itself into a sphere, but not enough to clear the path of its orbit of other objects.

Eclipse: An obstruction of light caused by the alignment of astronomical objects. For example, a lunar eclipse is when the moon passes through the Earth's shadow.

Galaxy: Enormous collections of stars, gas, and dust, separated from each other by vast areas of relatively empty space. Our solar system is part of a galaxy we call the Milky Way.

Light Curve: A plot showing the brightness of a star over time. Scientists use the plots to study the behavior of variable stars.

Light Pollution: Excessive, misdirected, or obtrusive artificial light. Light pollution interferes with astronomy.

Light-year: The distance that light travels in one year—nearly 6 trillion miles. It is a standard unit of measuring the enormous distances between stars.

Luminosity: The amount of light emitted by an object, such as a star.

Magnitude: The brightness of a celestial object. Brighter objects are assigned lower numbers, and the brightest objects are given negative numbers.

Maria: The dark areas on the moon; the word comes from Latin (*mare* means sea).

Messier Object: A list of deep sky objects created by comet hunter Charles Messier in the late 1700s to keep track of objects that falsely resembled comets. Many of the most famous deep sky objects are known by their Messier designation—a capital M, followed by a number.

Meteor: A small piece of rock, ice, dust, or other debris falling to Earth from space and glowing white-hot from friction with the Earth's atmosphere.

Milky Way: Our home galaxy, made up of an estimated 200 billion stars. The light of billions of distant stars blend together to form an irregular band of soft light in our night sky.

Moon: A natural satellite orbiting a planet, dwarf planet, or asteroid. Also the proper name for the Earth's only natural satellite.

Nebula: A giant cloud of gas and dust in space. A few, such as the Orion Nebula, are visible to the naked eye.

Orbit: The path followed by an object, such as a planet, as it revolves around another object, such as the sun.

Parallax: How an object's position changes depending on an observer's position; by comparing the difference in position at two different times, astronomers can use parallax to determine distance.

Period: The time for one complete cycle of a regularly recurring event, such as a single orbit of a planet, or the brightening and dimming of a variable star.

Planet: An object orbiting around a star that has enough gravity to compress itself into a sphere and clear its orbit of other objects. Our solar system has eight known planets, including the Earth. Five of the other seven are easily visible to the naked eye.

Satellite: An object in orbit around another object. Usually refers to a natural or synthetic object in orbit around a planet, dwarf planet, or asteroid.

Spectrum: A band of colors, as seen in a rainbow, produced by passing light through a prism to separate different wavelengths.

Standard Candle: A celestial object with a known luminosity, used to measure cosmic distances.

Star: A massive ball of super-hot plasma, primarily hydrogen, that emits light and heat from nuclear fusion taking place in its core.

Star cluster: A group of stars bound together gravitationally and moving together through space. There are two kinds of star clusters. Globular clusters are ancient associations of stars that orbit around the galactic core. Open clusters are groups of relatively young stars within the galactic disk that share a common origin.

Sun: Our home star and the center of our solar system.

Telescope: An optical instrument that makes it easier to observe dim, distant objects. Telescopes gather and focus light, making objects appear brighter. The larger the light gathering opening (aperture) of a telescope, the brighter the objects in it will appear. Aperture and optical quality, rather than magnification (or "power"), determine what can be seen through a telescope.

Twilight: The period of time when the sun is below the horizon but still lights the sky.

Variable Star: A star or star system that fluctuates in brightness over a timescale of hours to years.

Additional Reading, Resources, and Community Science

WEBSITES

WWW.AAVSO.ORG

Home of the American Association of Variable Star Observers, where you can learn how to observe variable stars and report your observations for scientific research.

WWW.AMSMETEORS.ORG

Home of the American Meteor Society, including tips for observing meteors and reporting your observations for scientific research.

WWW.ASTROLEAGUE.ORG

Home of the Astronomical League, the umbrella organization for over 240 local astronomy clubs located across the United States. The league also offers a range of services to amateur astronomers who don't have a local club.

HTTPS://DARKSITEFINDER.COM

Dark Sky Finder provides light pollution maps that can help you find good locations for stargazing.

WWW.DARKSKY.ORG

Home of the International Dark-Sky Association, where